- Selenophile -
A person who loves
the moon.

- Cat -
Curiosity and the
mysteries of the moon.

FULL COLOR

Planner for A Magical

2023

Amy Cesari

Be a fire-safe witch!

Lots of space above
and around the flame. →

Candle is on a
fire-safe dish.

Never leave
flames unattended.

This Book Belongs To:

- Thirteen Moons -

Pull tarot cards, cast rune stones, or write your own words of wisdom for each moon of the year. Fill them all out at the beginning of the year, or do it moon-by-moon as a "look ahead" or a reflection of what's passed.

JULY
7

AUGUST
8

BLUE MOON
AUGUST
9

SEPTEMBER
10

OCTOBER
11

NOVEMBER
12

DECEMBER
13

A full moon ritual is called an Esbat.

The Magic is in Your Hands.

The moon is comforting and familiar, yet mysterious and full of possibility. Moon magic isn't about becoming the best version of yourself, but about accepting all phases—dark to light—as essential pieces of you.

Much of the moon's power lies in a subtle energy where "all is well." But the moon is also about experiencing growth, change, and new phases in a continuous cycle.

The most widely accepted definition of magic is the ability to influence your destiny. To harness intention, will, and the natural forces around you—such as the moon, the sun, the planets, and the changing seasons—is magic.

Magic is like an invisible thread. You may barely notice it's there at times. But if you hang onto that thread of intention (and action) through the many moons and phases of life, that magic will come through for you in life-changing ways.

This book isn't about planning to do more, but about prioritizing magic in your life and pulling that thread throughout the entire year. So imagine yourself in a feeling-place where nothing is wrong and there's nothing to fix. You've already got what you need to make this year magical. Are you ready? Say yes!

Using Your "Moon Child" Intuition

Witches and mystics have associated intuition, moon magic, and the watery depths of the subconscious for thousands of years. So how do you actually use your intuition and the moon's magic? Here's the secret (Try it now! It works!)

1. Close your eyes and imagine that you are the moon. Then look down on your physical self, a little "moon child" here on earth. Pause for a moment and just observe your human self from the perspective of the moon.

2. Let the moon see all of your feelings, dark and light. Let it see your insecurities, flaws, worries, fears, whatever you've got going on, and lay it out on the moon table.

3. From outside of yourself—from the moon's perspective—what does the moon see? What wisdom does the loving and accepting moon have for you, a perfect moon child in all phases, from dark to light?

The moon sees you without judgment—always. To love and accept the phases of the moon is to love and accept yourself in all phases, too.

When you see yourself as the moon sees you, you'll begin an upward spiral of energy, raising your spirit so you feel a little bit more magical, hopeful, curious, capable, or clear.

The moon's endless cycles represent the many new chances you have to try again, to feel a little better, or to reinvent yourself all over. When you know that it's "just a phase" to have both dark and light, you can hold on to that thread of intention and keep your magic growing by the phases of the moon.

Wield Thy Power!
Moon Child, the Magic Is Yours.

THE MOON MADE ME DO IT

Tips to Use this Planner

1. Familiarize yourself with the introduction and basics of "moon magic."
2. Fill out the "MOON VISION" and "MOON QUEST" planning pages in the intro.
3. Aim to stay in sync with the phases of the moon, even if it's "just a little." And try to perform the "big spell" or one of the mini spells in this book each month.
4. Review your "MOON VISION" each month or new moon. Adjust as needed, then break your goals into smaller intentions and actions for the month.
5. Repeat this process for as many of the 12 months of the year as you can to "stir the cauldron"... and see what happens. Are you ready for magic?! *(Yes!)*

• Write in this book! Take notes. Expressing your thoughts in writing is a powerful way to create your reality. Here are some ideas of what to write: *Your day-to-day-mundane appointments. Daily gratitude. Daily reflections. Daily tarot. A diary of your spiritual journey. Intuitive messages. How you feel during different moon phases.*

• "Spellcasting Basics" are included to show you how to cast a circle, ground and center, and perform a "full" spell. If you are new to spells, please be sure to read this.

• Always remember, the magic is inside you. Even if you start this book "late" in the year, or if it isn't "the best" moon phase, you are the most powerful force in your own life. The seasons, sun, and moon are just tools to help you unlock the magic within.

Goals, Plans, and Intentions

Yes, this is a planner, but that doesn't mean you have to get intense about... planning. You can even plan to do less this year. In fact, that's a great idea. Get to know what *you* want (not your family, not society, etc...) and then use the powers of the moon to focus your energy on those things. Here are some tips:

• Less is more. Go for broader feelings and intentions rather than super specific dates, processes, and outcomes. Leave room for magic to surprise you in fantastic ways.

• Make your goals as big or small as you want.

• Instead of saying what you don't want, "to stop being an emotional wreck," phrase it positively so you feel good when you say it, "to feel at ease with my emotions."

• Any plans you make are more of a guideline. Don't be afraid to scrap them and do something else if they don't feel right anymore. It's never too late to change directions or make new plans—in fact, that's often where the best moon magic comes in.

MOON MAGIC
The Big Picture

The Sun

The moon was likely created by the debris from a large object crashing into earth. And so the moon is actually a part of "us" (the earth) and also part of the cosmos—As Above, So Below.

The moon is a gravitational counterbalance to the earth. Its presence helps to steady out the climate and seasons, and the moon has played an important part of life's evolution on the planet.

The gravitational pull of the moon also causes the land and water to bulge on two sides of the earthly sphere. We call this phenomenon "the tides." You've probably witnessed the water's tides, but there is also a land tide that literally causes the earth's crust to bulge a few centimeters or more.

In theory, the moon's gravity also affects people, plants, and animals on the earth.

The moon "pushes and pulls" on the energy, water, and "tides" in our bodies and can affect our moods, energy levels, and subconscious—

You Are Here*
*APPROXIMATELY

New Moon

Full Moon

*Not quite to scale!
(& UNFATHOMABLY BIGGER)

therefore making the moon a powerful and plentiful force to use in magic.

And although the moon is often the brightest light in the night sky, it doesn't illuminate itself. The moon reflects the light of the sun.

You can use this metaphorical power to look at your own reflection, viewing yourself from a top-down perspective of intuition. (See the previous "Moon Child Intuition" exercise.)

You can also use this reflective magic to work with manifestation and the law of attraction: what you "reflect" as feelings, energy, and emotion can and will influence your physical reality—As Above, So Below.

For these reasons and more, people have worshiped the moon and likened it to divine power and magic for thousands of years.

Throughout this book, you'll work with the moon to find your own rhythm and reflection of light. *So... look up... Look at the moon!*

THE SECRETS OF

YOUR FEELINGS ARE THE SECRET SAUCE

To make real magic happen, combine actions (things that you do), intentions (also known as feelings or emotions), as well as powers outside of yourself, such as the moon and nature. This chart will give you some ideas on how to feel and set your intentions, while the next chart will cover actions. Both are essential ingredients to make your magic come alive.

An intention is when you strongly feel what you desire in your body, as if you already have it. And as the moon waxes and wanes, you'll "pull the thread" of magic forward by listening to your feelings and continually refocusing these intentions with actions to match.

Since the moon and emotions are both linked to the subconscious, *you'll use your body to feel these things and set intentions,* not your thoughts in your conscious mind.

FIRST QUARTER

Feel where you would like to change, grow, or expand. Allow yourself to dream and imagine what it might be like to make a change, even if it doesn't seem possible right now.

WAXING CRESCENT

Feel what excites you and sparks a sense of curiosity. Ask questions and look for answers, clues, patterns, and coincidences. Use the subtle feelings of what "lights you up" to set intentions and guide your actions.

NEW MOON

Allow yourself to feel where you are judging yourself. When you are ready, forgive yourself and let the energy shift until you find a place of neutrality and self-acceptance.

MOON MAGIC

Full Moon

Reaffirm your visions and intentions until the energy of what you desire begins to feel real.

If you feel clarity, make decisions to move forward quickly.

If you feel confusion, illuminate your emotions through writing, ritual, divination, movement, etc.

Ask: What am I missing? What am I feeling?

Last Quarter

Allow yourself to feel what's working, and what isn't. Let your feelings flow to a place of ease and trust in yourself, so you can discern what you want and what you do not want.

Waning Crescent

Feel the relief as you realize that some thoughts and feelings are unnecessary. Intend to let those things go, and then see what you have left. Let your intentions flow to a place of release.

Dark

Let the darkness filter out noise and distractions. Take a step back from actions and thoughts. Allow the dark moon to reset your mind, body, and spirit with the energy of rest.

Patchouli

WAXING GIBBOUS

This nearly-full moon is a powerful time to look closely at your plans for the moon phase and refine them. Cast spells for personal power, strength, and tenacity. Keep going. You've got this!

Nettle & Mint

FIRST QUARTER

A beautiful moon to take action, draw in lunar power, and cast spells to increase whatever you desire more of in your life.

Citrine

WAXING CRESCENT

Follow your curiosity to explore new things. Begin activities to transform yourself and grow.

Sage

NEW MOON

The time just before the first light of the moon is auspicious for new beginnings. Cast spells to start new things, refresh your altar or physical space, and dream, plan, or discover new desires and possibilities.

Thyme & Salt

START HERE

Rose Quartz - Self Love

MOON PHASES

Sandalwood & Rose

FULL MOON
The full moon provides clarity and energy. It's the phase with the brightest power, so it is an excellent time to cast spells of any kind or do activities that make you feel alive and powerful.

Moonstone

WANING GIBBOUS
This moon is still bright and energetic. An excellent time for deep creative work, studying, and gathering information.

Hyssop

LAST QUARTER
You may feel called to finish projects, clean house, or tidy-up during this phase. Work magic to clear, release, and let go.

Clary Sage

WANING CRESCENT
This crescent is an excellent time to rest, reflect, study, or draw upon your intuition to see what you may like to change or release.

Lavender

DARK MOON
As the moon's cycle comes to an end, this phase can bring about important insights during shadow work and meditation. Allow time to look within and know yourself better.

Jet

Wormwood

AND MOON SPELLS

MOON SPELLS

You can do powerful spells!

Fill a black or silver bowl with water

Or gaze at the surface of a lake, puddle, or calm sea

MOON WATER

Place water under the full or new moon. Add crystals, herbs, and oils if desired. Use this water to anoint yourself or your tools in ritual.

SCRYING & DIVINATION

Read tarot cards, gaze at the moon, or gaze at the reflection of the moon on water. Look for visual clues, patterns, or flashes of inspiration.

Start simply!

Use your talents!

ALTAR & CORRESPONDENCE

An altar is a place to bring the spiritual into the material world—As Above, So Below. Symbolism amplifies your magic and speaks to your subconscious on a deeper level than words or thoughts.

Discover symbolism that represents the full "you," dark and light—the true essence of yourself.

Incense & Oils

Use scents and the magical properties of herbs to help you visualize, clarify, release, and otherwise add power to your spells.

MOON BATHING

Bathe or shower (pour the ritual water over your head) to calm, cleanse, or energize your mind, body, and spirit.

AND RITUALS

Try moon magic tonight!

Candle Spells

Simply gaze at a candle flame, or use candles to enhance and energize your magic. Customize your candles with oils, herbs, colors, and carvings.

TEA & KITCHEN

Eat, drink, and be magical! Add magic to your daily life and use non-toxic herbs for teas, cooking rituals, and kitchen spells.

MANIFESTING & RELEASING

Use the new, waxing, and full moon phases to visualize and work towards what you wish to manifest or create in your life.

Use the full, waning, and dark moons to release, let go, connect to your intuition, and create space for change to manifest.

CLEARING & CHARGING

Use the moon's magic to calm or energize yourself, your ritual tools, your crystals, or your spells.

MEDITATION

Use the moon's phases to accept the ups and downs of life, and to connect to your intuition, deities, or inner wisdom.

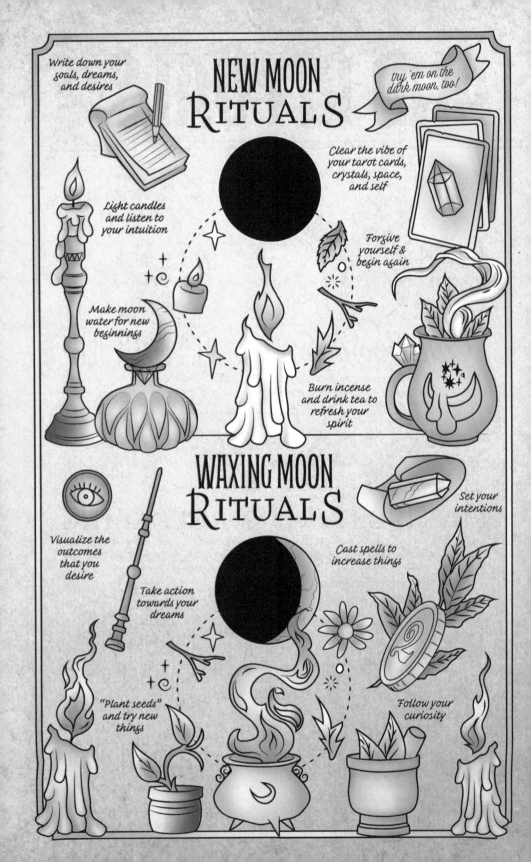

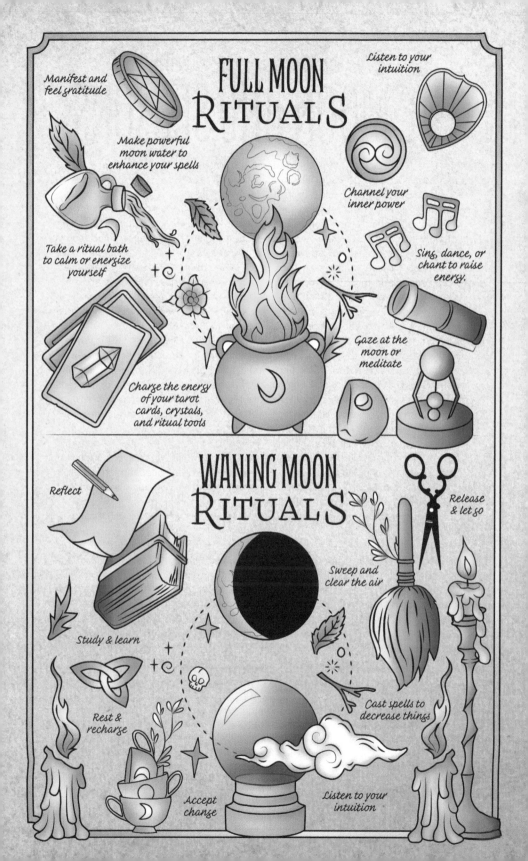

FULL MOON
RITUALS

Manifest and feel gratitude

Listen to your intuition

Make powerful moon water to enhance your spells

Channel your inner power

Take a ritual bath to calm or energize yourself

Sing, dance, or chant to raise energy.

Charge the energy of your tarot cards, crystals, and ritual tools

Gaze at the moon or meditate

WANING MOON
RITUALS

Reflect

Release & let go

Sweep and clear the air

Study & learn

Rest & recharge

Cast spells to decrease things

Accept change

Listen to your intuition

the correspondence of
THE MOON AND SEASONS

The moon completes a full cycle of its phases in just over 28 days, which is relatively quick. One moon cycle is perfect for shorter projects and immediate goals.

This book also relates the moon phases to a longer-term cycle, the seasons, also known as the Wheel of the Year, so you can use this longer cycle for longer-term goals and plans that'll take more than a month.

While the seasons and sun embody more of a conscious or outward energy, the moon is subconscious or internal. However, they both follow a similar cycle and progression of dark to light.

The handy chart on the following page demonstrates that the phases of the moon correspond to a similar energy point in the Wheel of the Year. This similar pattern of energy—the waxing and waning of light—is no coincidence. It's the pattern and flow of the creative force of the universe. This process and cycle is how magic "works" and what you'll cycle with in this book.

Here's an overview of the eight sabbats and a chart that connects them to the moon phases and seasons.

IMBOLC: February 1 or 2. Imbolc is the time to celebrate the first signs of spring, or the return of the sun's increasing light. This sabbat corresponds to the waxing crescent moon.

OSTARA: March 20. This sabbat is celebrated on the spring equinox. Witches often mark this day with a ritual planting of seeds. Ostara corresponds to the first quarter moon.

BELTANE: May 1. Beltane is a time for rituals of growth, creation, and taking action to make things happen. This sabbat corresponds to the waxing gibbous moon.

LITHA: June 20. This sabbat celebrates the summer solstice, when the sun is at its strongest. Litha is a time of great magical and personal power and corresponds to the full moon.

LUGHNASADH: August 1. This day is a celebration of the "first harvest" where we gather early grains, herbs, fruits, and vegetables from the earth. It corresponds to the waning gibbous moon, where light and power begin to descend from their fullest stage.

MABON: September 21. Celebrated on the autumnal equinox, this sabbat is about release, balance, and letting go. It is the second harvest and corresponds to the last quarter moon.

SAMHAIN: October 31. Samhain is a celebration of the dark half of the year. It is a time to cast spells of protection for the upcoming winter. It corresponds to the waning crescent moon.

YULE: December 21. Marked by the winter solstice and the shortest (darkest) day of the year, this sabbat corresponds to the dark and new moon.

A NOTE ABOUT THE CROSS QUARTER DATES AND SOUTHERN HEMISPHERE SEASONS:

CROSS QUARTER DATES: The dates for the two solstices and two equinoxes each year—Ostara, Litha, Mabon, and Yule—are calculated astronomically, from the position of the earth to the sun. The "cross quarter" festivals, which are the points between—Imbolc, Beltane, Lughnasadh, and Samhain—are often celebrated on "fixed" dates instead of the actual midpoints. This book lists both the "Fixed Festival Dates," where it's more common to celebrate, and the "Astronomical Dates." Choose either date or any time in between for your own ritual. 'Tis the season for magic.

SOUTHERN HEMISPHERE SEASONS: If you're on the "southern" half of the Earth, like in Australia, the seasonal shifts are opposite on the calendar year. So you'll feel the energy of the summer solstice (corresponding to the full moon) in December instead of June, and so on.

Your Moon Vision

AND PLANS FOR THIS YEAR:

Remember that plans almost always change. So try to envision what you can influence no matter what, and don't worry about deadlines. Magic works in its own time.

- Who do you want to be this year?
- What do you want this year to feel like?
- What do you want to take action on or work towards?
- What steps, thoughts, actions, and feelings will get you going in the direction that you desire?
- What does success feel and look like to you?
- What do you really want that you are hesitant to ask for?

Reach for the Moon

THINGS YOU CAN CONTROL: *Nothing!* You can't control anything, but you can influence, plan, and make things better for yourself and for the world. You matter, and your magic and energy matter.

THINGS YOU CAN INFLUENCE OR CHANGE: Your priorities, your actions, your thoughts, how you spend some of your time, the collective consciousness, and the spiritual evolution of the planet. Ultimately, you can influence how you feel after you've processed and felt all of your feelings just as they are.

YOUR MOON QUEST

Split up your MOON VISION into actions and feelings that will amplify and reflect your intentions. Correspond each of these actions or feelings to a moon phase (or season).

NEW MOON ACTIVITIES AND GOALS
(CORRESPONDS TO JANUARY & FEBRUARY)

How can you follow your curiosities, know yourself better, and start in a new direction, physically and energetically?

WAXING MOON ACTIVITIES AND GOALS
(CORRESPONDS TO MARCH, APRIL, AND MAY)

How can you take action and feel empowered? What do you need to feel and do to make your dreams and spells come true?

FULL MOON ACTIVITIES AND GOALS
(CORRESPONDS TO JUNE AND JULY)

How can you experience the fullest version of who you are right now?

WANING MOON ACTIVITIES AND GOALS
(CORRESPONDS TO AUGUST, SEPTEMBER, OCTOBER)

What can you release? How can you allow ease and trust in yourself?

DARK MOON ACTIVITIES AND GOALS
(CORRESPONDS TO NOVEMBER & DECEMBER)

How can you rest and go within? What can you do to refresh?

MOON SIGNS
The Moon in the Zodiac

Alongside the moon's phases, our moon travels through the zodiac constellations in about 28 days. The moon transits through each individual zodiac sign for about two or three days. You can use these short cycles to hyper-focus your magic and intentions, if you wish.

You'll often hear the moon sign called out (full moon in Scorpio!) and the moon's transits are noted on the weekly calendars in this book.

Use these pages as a handy reference sheet to see if you can feel the intricacies of the moon as it transits through the zodiac signs.

MOON IN ARIES

A fire sign, the moon in Aries evokes a desire to start fresh. You may find you've got extra energy to get things done and start new projects. However, this moon is a better time to start (and complete) short-term projects rather than long-term projects or planning. Channel energy or frustrations into movement and child-like activities—art, sports, or other playful activities that you enjoy.

MOON IN TAURUS

An earth sign and the zodiac sign symbolizing the home, comfort, decor, and finances. The moon in Taurus is an optimal moon sign for starting long-term projects. You may feel called to spend time at home, in your garden, or in nature. This moon sign is an excellent time to ground yourself by meditating or contemplating your desires outdoors.

MOON IN GEMINI

An air sign, the moon in Gemini is an excellent time for thinking, learning, reading, pursuing curiosities and interests, focusing on mental activities, traveling, and talking with fascinating people. You may find that journaling or discussing deep topics with others will lead to rewarding insights and new perspectives when the moon is in Gemini.

MOON IN CANCER

A water sign, the moon in Cancer is a time to be at home, reflect, and get in touch with your feelings. You may feel called to focus on bonding with family or loved ones in intimate ways. Cooking and cleaning may be more appealing when the moon is in Cancer. Activities in or near water, like swimming or walking along the shore, can help you get in tune with your watery emotions.

MOON IN LEO

A fire sign, the moon in Leo is a time to focus on yourself and your creativity. It's a magical time to get in touch with your own intuition and listen for what your heart truly desires. Do, say, and be who you are without fear. Let yourself shine and take time to live, laugh, and love as passionately as you can. This moon sign can be an excellent time for dating. However, you may also prefer to spend it all on yourself.

MOON IN VIRGO

Virgo is the earth sign associated with organization, efficient habits, and health. A moon in Virgo is undoubtedly the best time to start a new routine or positive habit, or to organize, get on a schedule, or tidy things up. You may find that your mind is sharp, sensitive, and quick while the moon is in Virgo, so take this opportunity to catch up on your studies, read, or learn new things.

MOON IN LIBRA

An air sign of diplomacy, balance, and visual appeal. The moon in Libra can be an auspicious time to work on relationships, find balance, and socialize. You may also be called to let some things go, to regain harmony or release the weight of what holds you down while the moon is in Libra. The Libra moon is also a time to speak up, share, or write about topics you believe in.

MOON IN SCORPIO

A dark water sign, use the moon in Scorpio to "find" motivation, harness your own power, take control, and rid yourself of things that no longer serve you. You may find you've got the drive and power to work on your finances or speak your mind on things you typically are afraid to bring up. Use this moon time to pursue any of your passions or go deep into topics of importance.

MOON IN SAGITTARIUS

The fire sign of truth and visions, the moon in Sagittarius is a time to make long-term plans that take you in new directions, to think big, to use your imagination, and visualize a positive future. You may also want to plan a trip, do something you've always wanted to do, or speak your truth where you've held back.

MOON IN CAPRICORN

An earth sign, the moon in Capricorn is a time to focus on career, business, structure, careful use of resources, and practical achievement. You may also feel inspired to declutter, get rid of energy and possessions you no longer need, or to otherwise cut the excess and reprioritize what is truly important in your life.

MOON IN AQUARIUS

An air sign that symbolizes esoterica, freethinking, and personal freedom, the moon in Aquarius is an excellent time to expand your mind to find new, unexpected ideas and solutions. Think about what you can do to help humanity or how you can contribute to society. If you typically follow the pack, this is an auspicious time to go your own way.

MOON IN PISCES

The water sign of dreaming, psychic awareness, and intuition, the moon in Pisces is auspicious time for divination, reflection, mystical pursuits, and retreats into nature or water. The two fish of this sign signify the pull of our earthy desires vs. our spiritual pursuits, so take time to balance this with meditation, daydreaming, and getting in touch with your soul's calling.

PERSONAL MOON CYCLES

Not everyone experiences the cycles and phases of the moon in the same way. You may have your own energetic pattern that doesn't peak at the full moon, for example.

To figure out your own personal moon cycle and rhythm, keep a "moon journal" that details how you feel emotionally and energetically over several moons, until you notice your pattern.

A FEW OTHER THINGS TO KNOW ABOUT THE COSMOS...

VOID-OF-COURSE MOON

There are void-of-course spots in between the moon signs. In these transitional phases, when the moon is void of course, there is a period of low energy where you may feel drained and exhausted or have trouble making decisions. Stores and businesses are "unusually" quiet, and people experience difficulty working together. It's also best not to start new projects or meet new people during the moon's void-of-course.

Often, you don't notice any difference because the void of course can be short—just a couple of minutes. But sometimes these periods can be hours or days, and that's when the shift in energy is quite noticeable! Being aware of these spots will help you use this energy to your advantage.

To see where these void spots are on the weekly calendar pages, look for the black triangles: ▶ These black triangles mark the start of the moon void-of-course cycle. The void ends when the moon enters the next sign.

PLANETARY RETROGRADES

Retrogrades happen when the planets appear to be moving backwards in our sky. When this occurs, planetary energy may have the opposite effect as "normal," causing confusion, a sudden change of perspective, or a need to "re-look," "re-bel," or "re-treat" in their area of planetary influence. These occurrences are marked on the calendar pages, as it can be helpful to be aware of their possible effects.

MERCURY: Mercury rules communication, so you may experience problems with technology, messages, or conversations. When Mercury is retrograde, back up, double-check, and be extra careful with what you say and hear. Prepare to be confused.

VENUS: Venus rules love and beauty. Be cautious about romantic relationships, exes, and changes in your physical appearance during Venus retrograde. Don't make a drastic change with your haircut or commit to sudden decisions with love.

MARS: Mars rules power and success. Don't start something big and new when Mars is retrograde. Make sure to think through career or business decisions. You may feel particularly slow or unenergized.

JUPITER: Jupiter rules travel, expansion, higher education, and finance. During Jupiter retrograde, you may have issues with transportation or trouble making progress or "growing" your career and finances. It's a good time to slow down, make sure not to overspend, and take time to learn, study, and experiment.

SATURN: Saturn rules responsibility, structure, and discipline, and is often an illuminator of limitations. When Saturn goes retrograde, it gives you an opportunity to move past failure and see beyond boundaries and comfort zones.

NEPTUNE: Neptune rules illusion, dreams, spirituality, and fantasy. As these influences disappear during a retrograde, you may feel the stark reality of things you normally do not see. Use this time to re-examine the truth versus what you've been telling yourself, and find clues on how to bring dreams to reality.

URANUS: Uranus rules the unexpected, things involving change, liberation, and innovation. Uranus retrograde can push you to big realizations, where you can see past your limitations and fears. This retrograde can show you where you need to make changes.

PLUTO: Pluto rules the shadow and the underworld. During a Pluto retrograde, look at your shadow self and your needs for recognition, authority, and power. It's a good time to discover your shadow and find ways to work through the darkness.

PLANETARY RETROGRADES (℞) IN 2023:

Uranus ℞ begins August 24, 2022 and ends January 22, 2023.
Mars ℞ begins October 30, 2022 and ends January 12, 2023.
Mercury ℞ begins December 29, 2022 and ends January 18, 2023.
Mercury ℞ begins April 21, 2023 and ends May 14, 2023.
Pluto ℞ begins May 1, 2023 and ends Oct 10, 2023.
Saturn ℞ begins June 17, 2023 and ends Nov. 4, 2023.

Neptune ℞ begins June 30, 2023 and ends Dec 6, 2023.
Venus ℞ begins July 22, 2023 and ends Sept 3, 2023.
Chiron ℞ July 23, 2023 and ends Dec 26, 2023.
Mercury ℞ begins August 23, 2023 and ends Sept. 15, 2023.
Uranus ℞ begins August 28, 2023 and ends January 27, 2024.
Jupiter ℞ begins Sept. 4, 2023 and ends Dec. 30, 2023.
Mercury ℞ begins Dec 13, 2023 and ends Jan 1, 2024.

ECLIPSES

Eclipses happen when the sun or moon appears "blacked out" by a celestial shadow.

Eclipses always come in pairs and in opposite signs. A lunar eclipse in Taurus will follow a solar eclipse in Scorpio, for example.

A total lunar eclipse always coincides with a full moon and typically marks an energetic ending or culmination point. A total solar eclipse always coincides with the new moon and signifies a shift towards new beginnings.

If an eclipse's sign coincides with your own moon, rising, or sun sign—get ready for exciting events and turning points in your life.

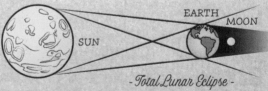

- *Total Lunar Eclipse* -

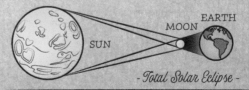

- *Total Solar Eclipse* -

ECLIPSES IN 2023:
Hybrid Solar Eclipse ♈ April 20
Penumbral Lunar Eclipse ♏ May 5
Annular Solar Eclipse ♎ Oct. 14
Partial Lunar Eclipse ♉ Oct. 28

SPELLCASTING BASICS

There are opening and closing steps that are basic accompaniments to spells in this book. These steps are optional but advisable: at least know "why" many witches perform these processes and try them out for yourself.

And keep in mind, this is a super basic "coloring book" guide to the spellcasting process. There are books and online sources that go much further in-depth.

THE SECRET OF SPELLS

The secret to powerful spells is in you. Your feeling and vibration in alignment with your true source of self—and/or a higher power—is what makes spells work.

The secret isn't in having the right ingredients and doing all the steps in a particular order. It's in your ability to focus your intent and use your feelings, mind, and soul to call in what you want—to harness the energy of yourself in harmony with the Earth, stars, moon, planets, or whatever other spiritual forces you call upon.

BREAK THE RULES

The first rule is to throw out any of the rules that don't work for you. Do things that feel right, significant, and meaningful. Adapt spells from different practices, books, and teachers. The only way to know what works is to follow your curiosity and try things out.

USING TOOLS

Your feelings and vibration are what unlocks the magic, not the tools, exact words, or sequences. You can cast amazing spells for free with no tools at all, and you can cast an elaborate spell that yields no results.

That said, tools like herbs, oils, crystals, and cauldrons can be powerful and fun to use in your spells. Just don't feel pressured or discouraged if you don't have much to start. Keep your magic straightforward and powerful. The right tools and ingredients will come.

"AS ABOVE, SO BELOW"

Tools, ingredients, and symbols are based on the magical theory of sympathetic magic and correspondence. You might hear the phrase, "As Above, So Below," which means the spiritual qualities of objects are passed down to earth. It's "sympathetic magic," or "this equals that," like how a figure of a lion represents that power but is not an actual lion.

Start by following lists, charts, and spells to get a feel for what others use and then begin to discover your own meaningful symbolism and correspondences.

PERMISSION

Spellbooks are like guidelines. They should be modified, simplified, or embellished to your liking. And don't degrade your magic by calling it "lazy." Keeping your witchcraft simple is okay. Go ahead, you have permission.

Also, it's not a competition to see who can use the most esoteric stuff in their spell. Hooray! It's about finding your personal power and style.

SPELLCASTING OUTLINE:

1. Plan and prepare.
2. Cast a circle.
3. Ground and center.
4. Invoke a deity or connection to self.
5. Raise energy.
6. Do your spellcraft (like the spells in this book).
7. Ground and center again.
8. Close your circle.
9. Clean up.
10. Act in accord (and be patient!).

1. PLAN AND PREPARE: If you're doing a written spell, read it several times to get familiar with it. Decide if there's anything you'll substitute or change. If you're writing your own spell, enjoy the process and mystery of seeing the messages and theme come together.

Gather all of the items you'll be using (if any) and plan out space and time where you'll do the spell. Spells can be impromptu, so preparations can be quick and casual if you like.

2. CAST A CIRCLE AND CALL THE QUARTERS: A magic circle is a container to collect the energy of your spell. Circles are also protective, as they form a ring or "barrier" around you. Circles can elevate your space to a higher vibration and clear out unwanted energy before you begin. Calling the Quarters is done to get the universal energy of the elements flowing. Incense is typically burned at the same time to purify the air and energy. If you

can't burn things, that's ok. If you've never cast a circle, try it. It's a mystical experience like no other. Once you have a few candles lit and start to walk around it, magic does happen!

HOW TO CAST A CIRCLE: This is a basic, bare-bones way to cast a circle. It's often much more elaborate, and this explanation barely does it justice, so read up to find out more. And note that while some cast the circle first and then call the Quarters, some do it the other way around.

1. Hold out your hand, wand, or crystal, and imagine a white light and a sphere of pure energy surrounding your space, as you circle around clockwise three times. Your circle can be large or it can be tiny, just space for you and your materials.

2. Call the Four Quarters or Five Points of the Pentagram, depending on your preferences. The Quarters (also known as the Elements!) are Earth (North), Air (East), Fire (South), and Water (West). Many use the Pentagram and also call the 5th Element, Spirit or Self.

Face in each direction and say a few words to welcome the element. For example, "To the North, I call upon your power of grounding and strength. To the East, I call upon the source of knowledge. To the South, I call upon your passion and burning desire to take action. To the West, I call upon the intuition of emotion. To the Spirit and Source of Self, I call upon your guidance and light."

3. GROUND AND CENTER: Grounding and centering prepare you to use the energy from the Earth, elements, and universe. Most witches agree that if you skip these steps, you'll be drawing off of your own energy, which can be exhausting and ineffective. It's wise to ground and center both before and after a spell. It's like the difference between being "plugged into" the magical energy of the Earth and universe versus "draining your batteries."

HOW TO GROUND AND CENTER:

To ground, imagine the energy coming up from the core of the Earth and into your feet, as you breathe deeply. You can visualize deep roots from your feet all the way into the center of the Earth, with these roots drawing the Earth's energy in and out of you. The point is to allow these great channels of energy to flow through you and into your spell. You can also imagine any of your negative energy, thoughts, or stress leaving.

To center, once you've got a good flow of energy from the ground, imagine the energy shining through and out the top of your head as a pure form of your highest creative self and then back in as the light of guidance. Suspend yourself here between the Earth and the sky, supported with the energy flowing freely through you, upheld, balanced, cleansed, and "in flow" with the energy of the universe. This process takes just a couple of minutes.

4. INVOKE A DEITY OR CREATIVE SOURCE: If you'd like to invoke a deity or your highest self to help raise energy and your vibration, call upon them. Invoking deities is way deeper than this book, so research it more if it calls to you!

5. RAISE ENERGY: The point of raising energy is to channel the universal (magical!) forces you tapped into through the previous steps to use in your spell. And raising energy is fun. You can sing, dance, chant, meditate, or do breath work. You want to do something that feels natural, so you can really get into it, lose yourself, and raise your state of consciousness.

A good way to start is to chant "Ong," allowing the roof of your mouth to vibrate ever so slightly. This vibration changes up the energy in your mind, body, and breath and is a simple yet powerful technique.

Another tip is to raise energy to the point of the "peak" where you feel it at its highest. Don't go too far where you start to tucker out or lose enthusiasm!

6. DO YOUR SPELL: Your spell can be as simple as saying an intention and focusing on achieving the outcome of what you want, or it can be more elaborate. Whichever way you prefer, do what feels right to you.

TIPS ON VISUALIZATION AND INTENTION:

Most spellwork involves a bit of imagination and intention, and here are some subtleties you can explore.

The Power of You The most important tool in magic is you. You've got it—both power right now and vast untapped power that you can explore. To cast a successful spell, you've got to focus your mind and genuinely feel the emotions and feelings of the things you want to manifest.

If you haven't started meditating in some form yet, start now! It's not too late, and it's easier than you think.

Visualize the Outcome

Visualization doesn't have to be visual. In fact, *feeling* the outcome of what you want may be more effective than seeing it (try both). And try to feel or see the *completion* of your desire without worrying about the process or *how* you'll get there.

If you don't know how you're going to achieve your goal (yet!) it can feel overwhelming when you try to visualize how you're going to pull it off. Instead, feel the sense of calm, completion, and control that you'll feel *after* you achieve it.

Phrase it Positively

Another tip is to phrase your intentions and desires positively. You're putting energy into this, so make sure the intention is going to be good for you. Instead of saying what you don't want, "to get out of my bad job that I hate," phrase it positively, "I want to do something that's fulfilling with my career."

Then you'll be able to feel good about it as you visualize and cast your spell.

7. GROUND AND CENTER AGAIN

After your spell, it's important to ground out any excess energy. Do this again by visualizing energy flowing through you and out. You can also imagine any "extra" energy you have petering out as you release it back into the Earth.

8. CLOSE YOUR CIRCLE

If you called the Quarters or a deity, let them know the spell has ended by calling them out again, with thanks if desired.

Close your circle the opposite of how you opened it, circling around three times or more counterclockwise. Then say, "This circle is closed," or do a closing chant or song to finish your spell.

9. CLEAN UP

Don't be messy with your magic! Put away all of your spell items.

10. ACT IN ACCORD: Once you have cast your spell, you've got to take action. You can cast a spell to become a marine biologist, but if you don't study for it, it's never going to happen. So take action towards what you want to open the possibility for it to come.

Look for signs, intuition, and coincidences that point you in the direction of your desires. If you get inspired after a spell, take action! Don't be surprised if you ask for money and then come up with a new idea to make money. Follow those clues, especially if they feel exciting and good.

If your spell comes true, discard and "release" any charm bag, poppet, or item you used to hold and amplify energy. Also, give thanks (if that's in your practice) or repay the universe in some way, doing something kind or of service that you feel is a solid trade for what you received from your spell.

WHAT IF YOUR SPELL DOESN'T WORK?

It's true that not all spells will work! But sometimes the results just take longer than you'd like, so be patient.

If your spell doesn't work, you can use divination or meditation to do some digging into reasons why.

The good news is your own magic, power, frequency, and intention is still on your side. You can try again and add more energy in the direction of your desired outcome by casting another spell.

Give it some deep thought. What else is at play? Did you really take inspired action? Are you totally honest with yourself about what you want? Are there any thoughts or feelings about your spell that feel "off"? Are you grateful for what you already have? Can you "give back" or reciprocate with service or energy?

FOR MORE TIPS AND INSPIRATION:

Seek out websites, books, podcasts, and videos on spirituality. Follow your intuition and curiosity to deepen your practice and find your own style. And check out other books in the *Coloring Book of Shadows* series, like the *Book of Spells* and *Witch Life*.

SOUTHERN HEMISPHERE MAGIC

If you're in the Southern Hemisphere in a place like Australia, there are a couple of differences that you'll need to note.

The biggest difference is that since seasonal shifts are opposite on the calendar year, you'll feel the energy of Samhain around May 1 instead of October 31.

Southern Hemisphere "spinning and circle casting" will go "sun wise" according to the south—counterclockwise for invoking (drawing in), clockwise for banishing (letting go).

North and South Elements are also typically swapped in Southern Hemisphere magic—North = Fire, South = Earth.

SO MOTE IT BE.

"HIS MOTHER WAS A WITCH, AND
ONE SO STRONG THAT COULD
CONTROL THE MOON."

William Shakespeare
The Tempest, Act V

1ST HALF 2023

January

S	M	T	W	Th	F	Sa
1	2	3	4	5	○	7
8	9	10	11	12	13	◐
15	16	17	18	19	20	●
22	23	24	25	26	27	◑
29	30	31				

February

S	M	T	W	Th	F	Sa
			1	2	3	4
○	6	7	8	9	10	11
12	◐	14	15	16	17	18
19	●	21	22	23	24	25
26	◑	28				

March

S	M	T	W	Th	F	Sa
			1	2	3	4
5	6	○	8	9	10	11
12	13	◐	15	16	17	18
19	20	●	22	23	24	25
26	27	◑	29	30	31	

April

S	M	T	W	Th	F	Sa
						1
2	3	4	5	○	7	8
9	10	11	12	◐	14	15
16	17	18	19	●	21	22
23	24	25	26	◑	28	29
30						

May

S	M	T	W	Th	F	Sa
	1	2	3	4	○	6
7	8	9	10	11	◐	13
14	15	16	17	18	◑	20
21	22	23	24	25	26	●
28	29	30	31			

June

S	M	T	W	Th	F	Sa
				1	2	○
4	5	6	7	8	9	◐
11	12	13	14	15	16	17
●	19	20	21	22	23	24
25	◑	27	28	29	30	

2ND HALF 2023

July

S	M	T	W	Th	F	Sa
						1
2	○	4	5	6	7	8
◑	10	11	12	13	14	15
16	●	18	19	20	21	22
23	24	◐	26	27	28	29
30	31					

August

S	M	T	W	Th	F	Sa
	○	2	3	4	5	
6	7	◑	9	10	11	12
13	14	15	●	17	18	19
20	21	22	23	◐	25	26
27	28	29	○	31		

September

S	M	T	W	Th	F	Sa
					1	2
3	4	5	◑	7	8	9
10	11	12	13	●	15	16
17	18	19	20	21	◐	23
24	25	26	27	28	○	30

October

S	M	T	W	Th	F	Sa
1	2	3	4	5	◑	7
8	9	10	11	12	13	●
15	16	17	18	19	20	◐
22	23	24	25	26	27	○
29	30	31				

November

S	M	T	W	Th	F	Sa
			1	2	3	4
◑	6	7	8	9	10	11
12	●	14	15	16	17	18
19	◐	21	22	23	24	25
26	○	28	29	30		

December

S	M	T	W	Th	F	Sa
					1	2
3	4	◑	6	7	8	9
10	11	●	13	14	15	16
17	18	◐	20	21	22	23
24	25	○	27	28	29	30
31						

The 12 monthly moon calendars (facing page) are a riff on the 15th century Book of Hours, Très Riches Heures du Duc de Berry.

VISION & INTENTION
Gather your power. You are whole.

REFLECTION
What's working for you? What's not?

GOALS & ACTIONS
What does your magic need from you?

INTUITION
Accept all phases of yourself & begin again.

Drink tea with cinnamon & ginger

THIS MONTH:

Full Moon in Cancer: January 6
Mars ℞ ends; January 12
Mercury ℞ ends: January 18
Sun enters Aquarius: January 20
New Moon in Aquarius: January 21
Uranus ℞ ends: January 22

- Rose Quartz -
Self-Love

Cook with
rosemary & salt

JANUARY

SELF ACCEPTANCE

Look at the moon to release the past
and accept yourself without judgment.
Eat moon-shaped snacks and feel whole.

Wish on a falling star

*Meditate with obsidian to explore peace in the
unknown and restore the spin of your sacral chakra.*

- Celestite -
Inner peace & the guidance within

New Moon Magic
A Ritual to Start Fresh

Perform this ritual on any new moon of the year or on the full moon in January.

The new moon (or new year) is a time to start fresh and allow yourself to begin again.

This moon phase corresponds to the month of January or deep winter. The energy of this season and moon suggests a desire for change, which becomes possible from a place of self-acceptance.

And that's the paradox of new beginnings: you're wishing for newness, but you won't find the power to change in something new. Your power is in the feeling of belonging just as you are, without changing a thing about yourself.

THINGS YOU'LL NEED: A dark space to sit in silence, outdoors if possible. Optional: Thirteen candles set in a circle to represent each of the moons for the year, or five candles for the elements air, earth, fire, water, and spirit. Earthy incense such as patchouli, cypress, or verbena.

CAST THE SPELL: Light your incense if desired. Allow yourself a moment in the pitch darkness. This darkness is a space where there is nothing to do, nothing to change, and nothing to fix. Imagine yourself floating in the darkness, slowing moving towards the feeling of self-acceptance. There is a part of the universe that wholly supports, loves, and cares for you, just as you are. Be patient—you will find it.

If you're using candles, light them one at a time in a clockwise manner, with the light of each candle amplifying the acceptance of yourself.

When you feel a shift to a sense of peace within yourself, you are ready for whatever you desire to do or be next.

JANUARY 2023

	SUNDAY	MONDAY	TUESDAY
	1	2	3
	8	9	10
	15	16	17
	22 ★Lunar New Year Begins	23	24
	29	30	31

WEDNESDAY	THURSDAY	FRIDAY	SATURDAY
4	5	6 Full Moon ○ ♋	7
11	12	13	14 Last Quarter ◑
		☉ Sun in Aquarius ♒	
18	19	20	21 New Moon ● ♒
25	26	27	28 First Quarter ◐
★ Imbolc (Fixed Date)		★ Imbolc 9:27 PM EST	
1	2	3	4

DECEMBER 2022/JANUARY 2023

MONDAY, DECEMBER 26, 2022
► Moon void of course begins 1:19 PM EST

TUESDAY, DECEMBER 27, 2022
Moon enters Pisces ♓ 2:34 AM EST

WEDNESDAY, DECEMBER 28, 2022

THURSDAY, DECEMBER 29, 2022
► Moon void of course begins 1:21 AM EST
Moon enters Aries ♈ 5:36 AM EST
First Quarter ◑ 8:20 PM EST

FORGIVE YOURSELF

FRIDAY, DECEMBER 30, 2022

SATURDAY, DECEMBER 31, 2022
► Moon void of course begins 7:44 AM EST
Moon enters Taurus ♉ 12:08 AM EST

SUNDAY, JANUARY 1, 2023

Moon Water
FOR EMOTIONAL HEALING
Place a moonstone and a drop of amber oil
in water. Set it under the full or new moon.

JANUARY 2023

MONDAY, JANUARY 2
► Moon void of course begins 5:16 PM EST
Moon enters Gemini Ⅱ 9:44 PM EST

TUESDAY, JANUARY 3

WEDNESDAY, JANUARY 4
► Moon void of course begins 7:08 PM EST

THURSDAY, JANUARY 5
Moon enters Cancer ♋ 9:15 AM EST

FRIDAY, JANUARY 6
Full Moon ○ ♋ 6:08 PM EDT

SATURDAY, JANUARY 7
► Moon void of course begins 5:23 PM EST
Moon enters Leo ♌ 9:40 PM EST

SUNDAY, JANUARY 8

JANUARY 2023

MONDAY, JANUARY 9
► Moon void of course begins 8:52 PM EST

TUESDAY, JANUARY 10
Moon enters Virgo ♍ 10:15 AM EST

WEDNESDAY, JANUARY 11

THURSDAY, JANUARY 12
► Moon void of course begins 6:06 PM EST
Moon enters Libra ♎ 9:56 PM EST
♂℞ Mars Retrograde ends

FRIDAY, JANUARY 13

SATURDAY, JANUARY 14
Last Quarter ☽ 9:10 PM EST

SUNDAY, JANUARY 15
► Moon void of course begins 3:40 AM EST
Moon enters Scorpio ♏ 7:08 AM EST

Bay - Clear Visions
Benzoin - Accepting Emotions

JANUARY 2023

MONDAY, JANUARY 16

TUESDAY, JANUARY 17
▸ Moon void of course begins 9:27 AM EST
Moon enters Sagittarius ♐ 12:33 PM EST

WEDNESDAY, JANUARY 18
☿℞ Mercury Retrograde ends

THURSDAY, JANUARY 19
▸ Moon void of course begins 5:09 AM EST
Moon enters Capricorn ♑ 2:11 PM EST

FRIDAY, JANUARY 20
☉ Sun enters Aquarius ♒ 3:27 AM EST

SATURDAY, JANUARY 21
▸ Moon void of course begins 10:52 AM EST
Moon enters Aquarius ♒ 1:29 PM EST
New Moon ● ♒ 3:53 PM EDT

SUNDAY, JANUARY 22
Lunar New Year Begins
♅℞ Uranus Retrograde ends

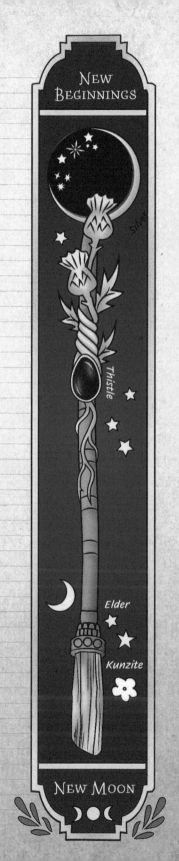

New Beginnings

Silver

Thistle

Elder

Kunzite

New Moon

JANUARY 2023

MONDAY, JANUARY 23
➤ Moon void of course begins 5:19 AM EST
Moon enters Pisces ♓ 12:36 PM EST

TUESDAY, JANUARY 24

WEDNESDAY, JANUARY 25
➤ Moon void of course begins 11:11 AM EST
Moon enters Aries ♈ 1:48 PM EST

THURSDAY, JANUARY 26

FRIDAY, JANUARY 27
➤ Moon void of course begins 4:01 PM EST
Moon enters Taurus ♉ 6:42 PM EST

SATURDAY, JANUARY 28
First Quarter ◑ 10:19 AM EST

SUNDAY, JANUARY 29

*Burn juniper, cedar, and lemon balm
to call on the energy of Artemis.*

JANUARY/FEBRUARY 2023

MONDAY, JANUARY 30
► Moon void of course begins 12:52 AM EST
Moon enters Gemini Ⅱ 3:35 AM EST

TUESDAY, JANUARY 31

WEDNESDAY, FEBRUARY 1
★ Imbolc (Fixed Festival Date)
► Moon void of course begins 6:58 AM EST
Moon enters Cancer ♋ 3:11 PM EST

THURSDAY, FEBRUARY 2

FRIDAY, FEBRUARY 3
★ Imbolc (Astronomical Date) 9:27 PM EST

SATURDAY, FEBRUARY 4
► Moon void of course begins 1:19 AM EST
Moon enters Leo ♌ 3:48 AM EST

SUNDAY, FEBRUARY 5
Full Moon ○ ♌ 1:29 PM EDT

ARTEMIS

*Greek Goddess
of the wild and
of the moon*

VISION & INTENTION
Gather your power. You are whole.

REFLECTION
What's working for you? What's not?

GOALS & ACTIONS
What does your magic need from you?

INTUITION
Accept all phases of yourself & begin again.

Drink mullein tea or burn it as incense to enliven your spirit.

THIS MONTH:

Imbolc: February 1-3
Full Moon in Leo: February 5
Sun enters Pisces: February 18
New Moon in Pisces: February 20

FEBRUARY
WEAVE AND SPIN
Look at the moon to follow your curiosities,
dream, and know yourself better.

Do activities that light your inner fire.

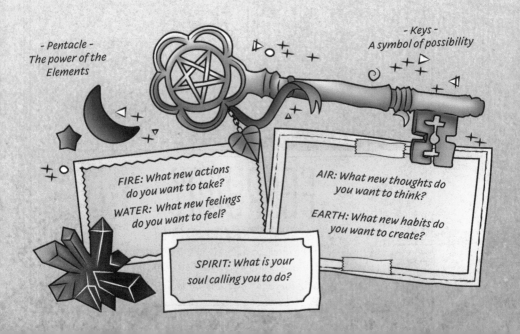

- Keys -
A symbol of possibility

- Pentacle -
The power of the Elements

FIRE: What new actions do you want to take?

WATER: What new feelings do you want to feel?

AIR: What new thoughts do you want to think?

EARTH: What new habits do you want to create?

SPIRIT: What is your soul calling you to do?

YOU HAVE THE KEYS

- Amethyst -
Serenity & spiritual
awareness

- Mint -
Enlivening your
spells with energy

- Quartz -
Transmuting energy
into physicality

WAXING CRESCENT MOON
A SLIVER OF LIGHT

Do this work on any waxing crescent moon or on the full moon in February (mid-winter).

The waxing crescent, when the moon's first sliver of light emerges, symbolizes the power of possibility and the magic of starting new things. This moon reminds us that nothing is permanent. You've always got the power to change.

The keys to unlocking "what's next" are often hidden "in the shadows." Perhaps you were called to art, spirituality, or botany, but you've buried those interests out of fear or to protect yourself.

Or maybe you're aware of these keys, but they seem like a random pile of shiny objects. Trust that they're not random. These pieces, parts, and shiny things all have a place in your life.

In this spell, you'll make an elemental key to guide you towards the new things you desire.

PREPARE: First, answer the "pentagonal key" questions on the opposite page. Don't overthink it. Trust your first inclinations without letting judgment or "the shadows" block the light.

Procure an actual key, or just write your answers on paper and use the paper as your key.

CAST THE SPELL: Hold your key under the moonlight until you feel the moonbeams shine within you. Then speak the answers to your key to set your intention. Anoint your key (optional) with a drop of basil oil or a sprig of basil.

Place the key under your pillow and sleep on it each night until the next full moon. Then keep your key in a special place—on your altar, in a charm bag, hung on the wall, around your neck, or blowing in the wind outdoors. This key will serve as an amulet of focus and power.

FEBRUARY 2023

	SUNDAY	MONDAY	TUESDAY
	29	30	31
	5 Full Moon ○ ♌	6	7
	12	13 Last Quarter ◑	14
	19	20 New Moon ● ♓	21
	26	27 First Quarter ◐	28

Moon Tea
TO ENERGIZE YOUR SPIRIT
Drink citrus & ginseng tea under the waxing crescent moon.

Light a gold candle. As it burns, focus your intentions on growing abundance.

WEDNESDAY	THURSDAY	FRIDAY	SATURDAY
★ Imbolc (Fixed Date) 1	2	★ Imbolc 9:27 PM EST 3	4
8	9	10	11
15	16	17	☉ Sun enters Pisces ♓ 18
22	23	24	25
1	2	3	4

FEBRUARY 2023

MONDAY, FEBRUARY 6
► Moon void of course begins 9:15 AM EST
Moon enters Virgo ♍ 4:14 PM EST

TUESDAY, FEBRUARY 7

WEDNESDAY, FEBRUARY 8

THURSDAY, FEBRUARY 9
► Moon void of course begins 1:40 AM EST
Moon enters Libra ♎ 3:47 AM EST

FRIDAY, FEBRUARY 10

SATURDAY, FEBRUARY 11
► Moon void of course begins 11:41 AM EST
Moon enters Scorpio ♏ 1:34 PM EST

SUNDAY, FEBRUARY 12

Anoint your broom with cinnamon oil and sweep clockwise (or left to right) to empower your spells.

FEBRUARY 2023

MONDAY, FEBRUARY 13
Last Quarter ◑ 11:01 AM EST
► Moon void of course begins 6:52 PM EST
Moon enters Sagittarius ♐ 8:31 PM EST

TUESDAY, FEBRUARY 14

WEDNESDAY, FEBRUARY 15
► Moon void of course begins 8:06 PM EST

THURSDAY, FEBRUARY 16
Moon enters Capricorn ♑ 12:00 AM EST

FRIDAY, FEBRUARY 17
► Moon void of course begins 11:18 PM EST

SATURDAY, FEBRUARY 18
Moon enters Aquarius ♒ 12:35 AM EST
☉ Sun enters Pisces ♓ 5:34 PM EST

SUNDAY, FEBRUARY 19
► Moon void of course begins 9:00 PM EST
Moon enters Pisces ♓ 11:56 PM EST

Sweep
counterclockwise
to release.

FEBRUARY 2023

MONDAY, FEBRUARY 20
New Moon ● ♓ 2:06 AM EST

TUESDAY, FEBRUARY 21
► Moon void of course begins 11:05 PM EST

WEDNESDAY, FEBRUARY 22
Moon enters Aries ♈ 12:14 AM EST

THURSDAY, FEBRUARY 23

FRIDAY, FEBRUARY 24
► Moon void of course begins 2:22 AM EST
Moon enters Taurus ♉ 3:29 AM EST

SATURDAY, FEBRUARY 25

SUNDAY, FEBRUARY 26
► Moon void of course begins 9:41 AM EST
Moon enters Gemini ♊ 10:48 AM EST

- Lapis Lazuli & Thyme -
Clarity of inner truth & the courage to listen.

FEBRUARY/MARCH 2023

MONDAY, FEBRUARY 27
First Quarter ◑ 3:06 AM EST

TUESDAY, FEBRUARY 28
► Moon void of course begins 8:07 PM EST
Moon enters Cancer ♋ 9:40 PM EST

WEDNESDAY, MARCH 1

THURSDAY, MARCH 2

FRIDAY, MARCH 3
► Moon void of course begins 9:22 AM EST
Moon enters Leo ♌ 10:16 AM EST

SATURDAY, MARCH 4

SUNDAY, MARCH 5
► Moon void of course begins 10:18 PM EST
Moon enters Virgo ♍ 10:38 PM EST

Use birch to make brooms, wands, and magical tools.

- Bow and Arrow -
Aiming from
your heart

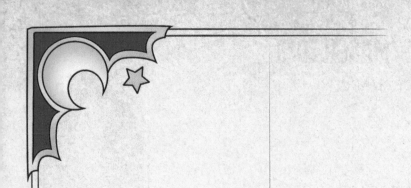

VISION & INTENTION
Gather your power. You are whole.

REFLECTION
What's working for you? What's not?

GOALS & ACTIONS
What does your magic need from you?

INTUITION
Accept all phases of yourself & begin again.

Gaze at a candle flame for
△ wisdom and energy.

THIS MONTH:

Full Moon in Virgo: March 7
Sun Enters Aries: March 20
Ostara (Spring Equinox): March 20
New Moon in Aries: March 21

MARCH

INTENTION

Look at the moon to set your intentions
and cultivate belief in yourself.
Deeply feel the outcome that you desire.

White, red, and black are traditional cord and candle colors to symbolize the waxing, full, and dark moon.

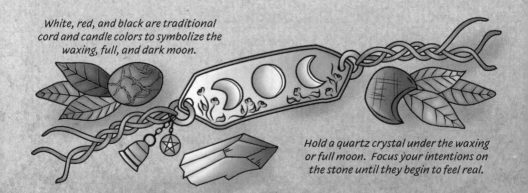

Hold a quartz crystal under the waxing or full moon. Focus your intentions on the stone until they begin to feel real.

Believe in Yourself

First Quarter Moon
A Knot Spell to Harness the Moon's Power

Perform this spell on a waxing moon, or on the full moon in March (early spring).

The waxing first-quarter moon embodies the energy of increasing power. This moon marks an auspicious time to focus your actions, nurture relationships, or "grow" whatever you wish.

Witches have used knot spells for hundreds (possibly thousands) of years. In Celtic lore, knots represent tying and untying of elemental powers, binding intention to the knot's creator.

THINGS YOU'LL NEED: A three-foot cord, one strand or three strands braided. Saltwater and an oil such as myrrh, olive, or eucalyptus.

CAST THE SPELL: Under the light of the moon, purify the cord with a sprinkle of saltwater, then anoint it with a drop of oil. Hold your cord up to the moon. Feel the lunar energy and light shining onto it and through your hands.

You'll tie either nine or thirteen knots into the cord, representing the nine phases of the moon or the thirteen moons of the year (your choice!).

Start with the first knot, and as you tie it, hold it up so you can see the moon through the loop that the knot creates. As you pull it closed, envision the moon power tying into the cord. Repeat for all but one knot, tying as evenly spaced as you can. For the 9th or 13th knot, tie the two ends together, or leave it loose as one long strand.

To use your moon cord, drape it around yourself or place it on your altar. Its presence will remind you of the power you have to change or create whatever you desire. You can also untie the knots when you need extra moon power. Repeat the spell and re-tie it to charge it again.

MARCH 2023

	SUNDAY	MONDAY	TUESDAY
	26	27	28
	5	6	7 Full Moon ○ ♍
	12	13	14 Last Quarter ◑
	19	★Ostara (Spring Equinox) ⊙ Sun enters Aries ♈ 20	21 New Moon ● ♈
	26	27	28 First Quarter ◐

Triple Goddess
MAIDEN-MOTHER-CRONE

The phases of life and of the moon

WEDNESDAY	THURSDAY	FRIDAY	SATURDAY
1	2	3	4
8	9	10	11
15	16	17	18
22	23	24	25
29	30	31	1

MARCH 2023

MONDAY, MARCH 6

TUESDAY, MARCH 7
Full Moon ○ ♍ 7:40 AM EST

WEDNESDAY, MARCH 8
► Moon void of course begins 9:07 AM EST
Moon enters Libra ♎ 9:44 AM EST

THURSDAY, MARCH 9

FRIDAY, MARCH 10
► Moon void of course begins 6:36 PM EST
Moon enters Scorpio ♏ 7:06 PM EST

SATURDAY, MARCH 11

SUNDAY, MARCH 12

*Pour a small offering of milk at a
forest crossroads to honor Diana.*

MARCH 2023

MONDAY, MARCH 13
► Moon void of course begins 2:58 AM EDT
Moon enters Sagittarius ♐ 3:21 AM EDT

TUESDAY, MARCH 14
Last Quarter ◑ 10:08 PM EDT

WEDNESDAY, MARCH 15
► Moon void of course begins 4:50 AM EDT
Moon enters Capricorn ♑ 8:06 AM EDT

THURSDAY, MARCH 16

FRIDAY, MARCH 17
► Moon void of course begins 10:14 AM EDT
Moon enters Aquarius ♒ 10:25 AM EDT

SATURDAY, MARCH 18

SUNDAY, MARCH 19
► Moon void of course begins 6:33 AM EDT
Moon enters Pisces ♓ 11:12 AM EDT

Diana

*Roman Goddess of
the hunt and
of the moon*

MARCH 2023

MONDAY, MARCH 20
★ Ostara (Spring Equinox) 5:24 PM EDT
☉ Sun enters Aries ♈ 5:24 PM EDT

TUESDAY, MARCH 21
► Moon void of course begins 11:58 AM EDT
Moon enters Aries ♈ 12:01 PM EDT
New Moon ● 1:23 PM EDT

WEDNESDAY, MARCH 22

THURSDAY, MARCH 23
► Moon void of course begins 2:42 PM EDT
Moon enters Taurus ♉ 2:42 PM EDT

FRIDAY, MARCH 24

SATURDAY, MARCH 25
► Moon void of course begins 12:19 PM EDT
Moon enters Gemini ♊ 8:42 PM EDT

SUNDAY, MARCH 26

- Sage -
Wisdom &
Wishes

- Moldavite -
Spiritual growth, rapid change, and
the wisdom of the earth & the cosmos.

MARCH/APRIL 2023

MONDAY, MARCH 27
▸ Moon void of course begins 9:39 PM EDT

TUESDAY, MARCH 28
Moon enters Cancer ♋ 6:22 AM EDT
First Quarter ◐ 10:32 PM EDT

WEDNESDAY, MARCH 29

THURSDAY, MARCH 30
▸ Moon void of course begins 9:45 AM EDT
Moon enters Leo ♌ 6:31 PM EDT

FRIDAY, MARCH 31

SATURDAY, APRIL 1

SUNDAY, APRIL 2
▸ Moon void of course begins 2:03 AM EDT
Moon enters Virgo ♍ 6:57 AM EDT

STAG

*Elemental Energy
& Growth*

VISION & INTENTION
Gather your power. You are whole.

REFLECTION
What's working for you? What's not?

GOALS & ACTIONS
What does your magic need from you?

INTUITION
Accept all phases of yourself & begin again.

- Sprouts -
Energy manifesting
in the physical realm

- Beryl -
Confidence in
beginning new things

THIS MONTH:

Full Moon in Libra: April 6
New Moon in Aries: April 20
Hybrid Solar Eclipse: April 20
Sun enters Taurus: April 20
Mercury ℞ : April 21 - May 14

APRIL

INSPIRED ACTION

Look at the moon to gather motivation
and energy to take action.

Light a silver candle to spark inspiration.

Wear or carry a citrine crystal to amplify your manifestations.

Eat or burn basil leaves to gather courage.

Stir clockwise during the waxing or full moon to create forward momentum.

Stir the Cauldron

Spells in Action
Moonbeams for Manifestation

Magic is often defined as the ability to influence your life through intention and will—but there is another essential part—action.

Keep in mind that action doesn't have to be... active. Rest and reflection are parts of the moon's cycle, so they're important steps for you, too.

Use this month to observe and stay in tune with the moon's cycle, gently "stirring the cauldron" in a continuous manner.

For a physical mechanism to help you along, focus on the intentions behind your spellwork as you stir your coffee or tea. Stir clockwise during the waxing and full moon, and counterclockwise during the waning and dark moon.

Watch how your stirring keeps spinning, even when you stop the action. This is just like periods of rest and reflection—the actions you've taken keep the spell moving—so there's no need to worry about momentum slowing down when you take a break or stop to reflect.

WAXING MOON: After the new moon, start putting new things in motion. Use what you learned during the last waning moon to guide you.

FULL MOON: When the full moon arrives, go over what you've accomplished and give yourself some credit. Celebrate your actions and magic.

WANING MOON: During the waning moon and into the dark moon, take time to rest, read, research, journal, and go inward. Reflect on whatever you're working on with your spells.

REPEAT: Repeat this cycle continuously to keep motion going between learning, resting, and taking actions. You'll "stir the cauldron" and keep your magic flowing with the power of the moon.

APRIL 2023

	SUNDAY	MONDAY	TUESDAY
	26	27	28 First Quarter ◑
	2	3	4
	9	10	11
	16	17	18
	23	24	25
	30	1	2

WEDNESDAY	THURSDAY	FRIDAY	SATURDAY
29	30	31	1
5	6 Full Moon ○ ♎	7	8
12	13 Last Quarter ◑	14	15
19	* Solar Eclipse ☉ Sun enters Taurus 20 New Moon ● ♈	21	22
26	27 First Quarter ◑	28	29
3	4	5 Full Moon ○ ♏	6

APRIL 2023

MONDAY, APRIL 3

TUESDAY, APRIL 4
▸ Moon void of course begins 9:50 AM EDT
Moon enters Libra ♎ 5:51 PM EDT

WEDNESDAY, APRIL 5

THURSDAY, APRIL 6
▸ Moon void of course begins 8:43 AM EDT
Full Moon ○ ♎ 12:35 AM EDT

*Send your prayers to the
gods on the smoke of incense
or on the steam of hot tea.*

FRIDAY, APRIL 7
Moon enters Scorpio ♏ 2:29 AM EDT

SATURDAY, APRIL 8

SUNDAY, APRIL 9
▸ Moon void of course begins 5:09 AM EDT
Moon enters Sagittarius ♐ 8:57 AM EDT

*Empower yourself with
nettle and peppermint.*

APRIL 2023

MONDAY, APRIL 10

TUESDAY, APRIL 11
► Moon void of course begins 6:48 AM EDT
Moon enters Capricorn ♑ 1:33 PM EDT

WEDNESDAY, APRIL 12

THURSDAY, APRIL 13
Last Quarter ◑ 5:11 AM EDT
► Moon void of course begins 10:14 AM EDT
Moon enters Aquarius ♒ 4:42 PM EDT

FRIDAY, APRIL 14

SATURDAY, APRIL 15
► Moon void of course begins 11:16 AM EDT
Moon enters Pisces ♓ 6:57 PM EDT

SUNDAY, APRIL 16

- Tiger's Eye - Confidence

Add dried hyssop to your mop water or broom to clear lingering energy.

APRIL 2023

MONDAY, APRIL 17
► Moon void of course begins 2:57 PM EDT
Moon enters Aries ♈ 9:09 PM EDT

TUESDAY, APRIL 18

WEDNESDAY, APRIL 19

THURSDAY, APRIL 20
► Moon void of course begins 12:13 AM EDT
New Moon ● ♈ 12:13 AM EDT
☉ Solar Eclipse 12:16 AM EDT
Moon enters Taurus ♉ 12:30 AM EDT
☉ Sun enters Taurus ♉ 4:13 AM EDT

FRIDAY, APRIL 21
► Moon void of course begins 11:41 PM EDT
☿℞ Mercury Retrograde April 21-May 14

- Moth -
Traveling between
light and dark

SATURDAY, APRIL 22
Moon enters Gemini ♊ 6:11 AM EDT

SUNDAY, APRIL 23

Bathe with lavender and peony petals
to enhance your psychic powers and
manifest your wishes.

APRIL 2023

MONDAY, APRIL 24
▸ Moon void of course begins 8:15 AM EDT
Moon enters Cancer ♋ 2:58 PM EDT

TUESDAY, APRIL 25

WEDNESDAY, APRIL 26
▸ Moon void of course begins 7:41 PM EDT

THURSDAY, APRIL 27
Moon enters Leo ♌ 2:30 AM EDT
First Quarter ◑ 5:20 PM EDT

FRIDAY, APRIL 28

SATURDAY, APRIL 29
▸ Moon void of course begins 6:53 AM EDT
Moon enters Virgo ♍ 2:59 PM EDT

SUNDAY, APRIL 30

INSPIRED ACTION

Citrine

Alder Wood

Beryl

Set intentions for
new adventures

WAXING MOON

VISION & INTENTION
Gather your power. You are whole.

REFLECTION
What's working for you? What's not?

GOALS & ACTIONS
What does your magic need from you?

INTUITION
Accept all phases of yourself & begin again.

Place a moonstone on your third eye.
Imagine moonbeams shining into your soul.

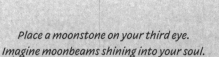

THIS MONTH:

Beltane: May 1-5th
Pluto Retrograde: May 1 - Oct 10
Penumbral Lunar Eclipse: May 5
Full Moon in Scorpio: May 5
Mercury ℞ : ends May 14
New Moon in Taurus: May 19
Sun enters Gemini: May 21

Periwinkle - Harnessing Witch Power

MAY

SHINE BRIGHTLY

Look at the moon to ignite your power,
gather magic, and live life on your own terms.

Cast a circle under the full moon and just sit in it.

Cast a circle with rose petals, elder
flowers, or hawthorn blossoms for
protection and spiritual energy.

- Patchouli -
Witch Power

- Malachite -
Bringing spiritual energy to earth

- Yarrow -
Magical Protection

You've Got the Magic.

WAXING GIBBOUS
A MOON MIRROR FOR PERSONAL POWER

Perform this spell during the waxing gibbous phase or on any full moon.

The waxing and full moons hold powerful energy. You can harness this moon magic by charging a "moon mirror." Moons and mirrors (or reflective surfaces like water or polished stone) have been used in magic for millennia. The moon's light is a reflection of the sun, as the moon produces no light of its own. And so, reflections are a potent form of moon magic.

THINGS YOU'LL NEED: A small round mirror. You can also use a polished stone or piece of metal. A container for the mirror that will obscure it from light, such as a dark cloth, bag, or box. If desired, embellish the container with embroidery, paint, or beads in lunar designs. A dark place and time where you can directly view the moon. An optional anointing oil or herb for power such as patchouli, cinquefoil, or mugwort.

PERFORM THE SPELL: With your mirror at the ready, cast a circle under the waxing or full moon's light. Hold the mirror up so you can see the moon reflected within. Rotate the mirror clockwise, either 3, 5, 9, or 13 times.

Use a drop of oil or sprig of herb and rub all the way around the edge of the mirror, clockwise, to consecrate and seal the spell. The mirror will be charged with the moon's power.

Place the mirror in the container, and do not let it see the light of day until you are ready to use it. When you're in need of personal power, intuitive guidance or resilience, gaze at your reflection in the mirror. Once you've used the mirror's magic, recharge it at the next waxing or full moon.

MAY 2023

"Man in the Moon"
*Many ancient cultures have legends of a
"man" or god's image in the moon.*

	SUNDAY	MONDAY	TUESDAY
		★ Beltane (Fixed Date)	
	31	1	2
	7	8	9
	14	15	16
	☉ Sun enters Gemini ♊ 21	22	23
	28	29	30

WEDNESDAY	THURSDAY	FRIDAY	SATURDAY
		Lunar Eclipse ♏ 12:11 AM ★ Beltane 2:13 PM EDT 5 Full Moon ○ ♏	
3	4	5 Full Moon ○ ♏	6
10	11	12 Last Quarter ◑	13
17	18	19 New Moon ● ♉	20
24	25	26	27 First Quarter ◐
31	1	2	3

MAY 2023

MONDAY, MAY 1
℞ Pluto Retrograde May 1 - Oct 10
★ Beltane (Fixed Festival Date)
► Moon void of course begins 7:53 PM EDT

TUESDAY, MAY 2
Moon enters Libra ♎ 2:09 AM EDT

WEDNESDAY, MAY 3

THURSDAY, MAY 4
► Moon void of course begins 5:17 AM EDT
Moon enters Scorpio ♏ 10:32 AM EDT

FRIDAY, MAY 5
Penumbral Lunar Eclipse in Scorpio ♏ 1:22 PM EDT
Full Moon ○ ♏ 1:34 PM EDT
★ Beltane (Astronomical Date) 2:13 PM EDT

SATURDAY, MAY 6
► Moon void of course begins 10:38 AM EDT
Moon enters Sagittarius ♐ 4:04 PM EDT

SUNDAY, MAY 7

Help Mama Quilla during the lunar eclipse!
Make a lot of noise to scare off her attackers.

MAY 2023

MONDAY, MAY 8
► Moon void of course begins 4:28 PM EDT
Moon enters Capricorn ♑ 7:33 PM EDT

TUESDAY, MAY 9

WEDNESDAY, MAY 10
► Moon void of course begins 7:52 PM EDT
Moon enters Aquarius ♒ 10:05 PM EDT

THURSDAY, MAY 11

FRIDAY, MAY 12
Last Quarter ◑ 10:28 AM EDT
► Moon void of course begins 11:15 PM EDT

SATURDAY, MAY 13
Moon enters Pisces ♓ 12:39 AM EDT

SUNDAY, MAY 14
☿℞ Mercury Retrograde ends
► Moon void of course begins 10:56 PM EDT

Quilla

*Inca Goddess
of the Moon*

MAY 2023

MONDAY, MAY 15
Moon enters Aries ♈ 3:56 AM EDT

TUESDAY, MAY 16

WEDNESDAY, MAY 17
► Moon void of course begins 5:10 AM EDT
Moon enters Taurus ♉ 8:28 AM EDT

THURSDAY, MAY 18

FRIDAY, MAY 19
New Moon ● ♉ 11:52 AM EDT
► Moon void of course begins 1:51 PM EDT
Moon enters Gemini ♊ 2:48 PM EDT

SATURDAY, MAY 20

SUNDAY, MAY 21
☉ Sun enters Gemini ♊ 3:09 AM EDT
► Moon void of course begins 6:12 PM EDT
Moon enters Cancer ♋ 11:28 PM EDT

Use a selenite wand and mugwort incense to move stagnant energy out of your house.

MAY 2023

MONDAY, MAY 22

TUESDAY, MAY 23

WEDNESDAY, MAY 24
► Moon void of course 5:12 AM EDT
Moon enters Leo ♌ 10:35 AM EDT

THURSDAY, MAY 25

FRIDAY, MAY 26
► Moon void of course begins 2:38 AM EDT
Moon enters Virgo ♍ 11:05 PM EDT

SATURDAY, MAY 27
First Quarter ◑ 11:22 AM EDT

SUNDAY, MAY 28

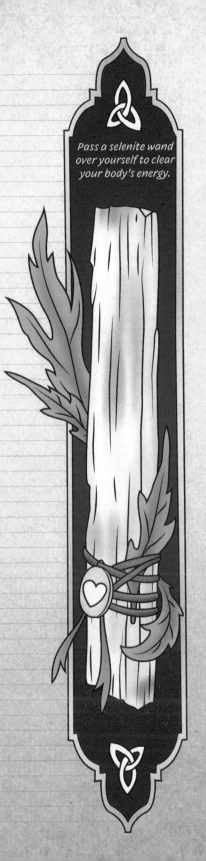

Pass a selenite wand over yourself to clear your body's energy.

MAY/JUNE 2023

MONDAY, MAY 29
► Moon void of course begins 5:46 AM EDT
Moon enters Libra ♎ 10:51 AM EDT

TUESDAY, MAY 30

WEDNESDAY, MAY 31
► Moon void of course begins 10:53 AM EDT
Moon enters Scorpio ♏ 7:45 PM EDT

THURSDAY, JUNE 1

FRIDAY, JUNE 2
► Moon void of course begins 8:51 PM EDT

SATURDAY, JUNE 3
Moon enters Sagittarius ♐ 1:03 AM EDT
Full Moon ○ 11:42 PM EDT

SUNDAY, JUNE 4
► Moon void of course begins 11:24 PM EDT

*Reflect the moon's light from water in a
silver bowl. Ask Selene for guidance.*

Selene

*A Greek Goddess
who personifies the
moon and
life's changes.*

VISION & INTENTION
Gather your power. You are whole.

REFLECTION
What's working for you? What's not?

GOALS & ACTIONS
What does your magic need from you?

INTUITION
Accept all phases of yourself & begin again.

- Cinquefoil & St. John's Wort -
Elemental Power

Harvest magical herbs
on the summer solstice.

THIS MONTH:

Full Moon in Sagittarius : June 3
Saturn ℞: June 17 - Nov. 4
New Moon in Gemini: June 18
Litha (Summer Solstice): June 21
☽ Sun Enters Cancer: June 21
▽ Neptune ℞: June 30 - Dec. 6

Blue Topaz

Aquamarine

JUNE

FULL STRENGTH

Look at the moon to feel the bright magic
and cosmic energy within yourself.

Celebrate how far you have come.

The Moon, she dances
Like the waves, like the waves on the shore
Making circles, making circles
Like the waves, like the waves on the shore

- Author Unknown

*(Find this chant on YouTube to
learn the simple melody.)*

THE FULL MOON
RITUAL OF DRAWING DOWN THE MOON

One of the most iconic full moon rituals is "Drawing Down the Moon." In theory, this simplified version of the ritual takes you to a trance state where you'll allow the moon goddess, god, or energy of the moon to be present within you.

If your practice is more secular or you aren't comfortable channeling a deity, you can call in the moon's energy as intuition, universal wisdom, or the power of your own divinity.

THINGS YOU'LL NEED: Plan to do this ritual under the light of the full moon. Going outdoors where you can see the moon is best, but you can perform it indoors at a window if necessary.

The only tool you need is your own body and spirit. However, many witches like to do this ritual with a tool—charging the tool with more moon power each time they perform it. This tool could be a crystal, a bowl or chalice of water, something made of silver, or whatever item represents the moon to you.

PERFORM THE RITUAL: Stand under the moon's light, holding your tool (if applicable). Feel the earth's energy grounding you down, coming up through your body, and steadying your presence. Then, gaze at the moon (if you can't see it, imagine it) until you feel its energy flow through you, bringing you to a peaceful, trance-like state. It may help to chant. Pick a favorite chant or use the example on the facing page.

Once you feel the fullness of the moon's power flowing through you, it's essential to let it shine back out. Visualize a bright orb coming out from the center of yourself and into a sphere around you, as if you have become the moon itself.

JUNE 2023

	SUNDAY	MONDAY	TUESDAY
	28	29	30
	4	5	6
	11	12	13
	18 New Moon ● ♊	19	20
	25	26 First Quarter ◑	28

THOTH

An Egyptian God of the moon, magic, writing, and wisdom.

WEDNESDAY	THURSDAY	FRIDAY	SATURDAY
31	1	2	3 Full Moon ○ ♐
7	8	9	10 Last Quarter ◑
14	15	16	17
21 ★Litha (Summer Solstice) ☉ Sun enters Cancer ♋	22	23	24
28	29	30	1

JUNE 2023

MONDAY, JUNE 5

TUESDAY, JUNE 6

WEDNESDAY, JUNE 7
▸ Moon void of course begins 12:40 AM EDT
Moon enters Aquarius ♒ 4:42 AM EDT

THURSDAY, JUNE 8

FRIDAY, JUNE 9
▸ Moon void of course begins 12:24 AM EDT
Moon enters Pisces ♓ 6:14 AM EDT

SATURDAY, JUNE 10
Last Quarter ◑ 3:31 PM EDT

SUNDAY, JUNE 11
▸ Moon void of course begins 9:20 AM EDT
Moon enters Aries ♈ 9:20 AM EDT

If clouds obscure the full moon, think of an obstacle that you face. Gaze towards the moon until the clouds part, and you'll receive a moonbeam of inspiration.

JUNE 2023

MONDAY, JUNE 12

TUESDAY, JUNE 13
► Moon void of course begins 2:27 PM EDT
Moon enters Taurus ♉ 2:31 PM EDT

WEDNESDAY, JUNE 14

THURSDAY, JUNE 15
► Moon void of course begins 9:36 PM EDT
Moon enters Gemini ♊ 9:46 PM EDT

FRIDAY, JUNE 16

SATURDAY, JUNE 17
♄℞ Saturn Retrograde June 17 - Nov. 4

SUNDAY, JUNE 18
New Moon ● ♊ 12:37 AM EDT
► Moon void of course begins 2:24 AM EDT
Moon enters Cancer ♋ 6:58 AM EDT

Egyptian God of the Moon

KHONSU

Honor Khonsu with offerings of bread, water, meat, & spices.

JUNE 2023

MONDAY, JUNE 19

TUESDAY, JUNE 20
➤ Moon void of course begins 5:43 PM EDT
Moon enters Leo ♌ 6:04 PM EDT

WEDNESDAY, JUNE 21
★ Litha (Summer Solstice) 10:58 AM EST
☉ Sun enters Cancer ♋ 10:58 AM EDT

THURSDAY, JUNE 22
➤ Moon void of course begins 1:01 PM EDT

FRIDAY, JUNE 23
Moon enters Virgo ♍ 6:35 AM EDT

SATURDAY, JUNE 24

SUNDAY, JUNE 25
➤ Moon void of course begins 6:24 PM EDT
Moon enters Libra ♎ 6:57 PM EDT

- Silver -
Moon Power

JUNE/JULY 2023

Moonstone may change colors depending on the moon phase and aura of the wearer.

MONDAY, JUNE 26
First Quarter ☽ 3:50 AM EDT

TUESDAY, JUNE 27

WEDNESDAY, JUNE 28
► Moon void of course begins 4:19 AM EDT
Moon enters Scorpio ♏ 4:55 AM EDT

THURSDAY, JUNE 29

FRIDAY, JUNE 30
► Moon void of course begins 10:20 AM EDT
Moon enters Sagittarius ♐ 10:59 AM EDT
♆℞ Neptune Retrograde June 30 - Dec. 6

SATURDAY, JULY 1

SUNDAY, JULY 2
► Moon void of course begins 9:33 AM
Moon enters Capricorn ♑ 1:20 PM EDT

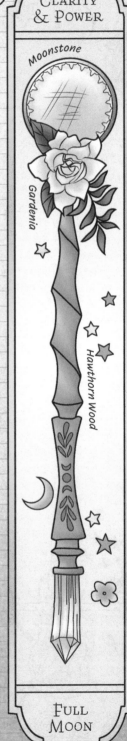

CLARITY & POWER

Moonstone

Gardenia

Hawthorn Wood

FULL MOON

VISION & INTENTION
Gather your power. You are whole.

REFLECTION
What's working for you? What's not?

GOALS & ACTIONS
What does your magic need from you?

INTUITION
Accept all phases of yourself & begin again.

THIS MONTH:

Full Moon in Capricorn: July 3
New Moon in Cancer: July 17
Sun Enters Leo: July 22
Venus ℞: July 22- Sept 3
Chiron ℞: July 23 - Dec 27

*The moon reflects memories of other lives.
Gaze at the moon to recall forgotten wisdom.*

*Friendship and the fullness
of the moon and sun.*

*Zinnias &
Dahlias*

JULY

CREATING MAGIC

Look at the moon to know yourself and
remember your soul's purpose.

Spend time and energy purely for pleasure.

Calm anxious full moon energy
by bathing with salt, valerian
root, skullcap, and lavender.

Invigorate your moon bath
or shower with bergamot,
vetivert, and Epsom salt.

HARNESSING THE FULL MOON
WORKING WITH UNWIELDY MOON ENERGIES

Have you ever felt sleepless, frustrated, or emotional at the full moon? Conversely, have you felt thrilled and bounding with energy?

The full moon typically amplifies what you've been feeling in the weeks prior, creating a surge of energy. While you can't control it, you can work with it. Here are a few ideas to try.

FOLLOW THE PHASES: No need to be perfect. A few actions each month make a big difference.

If you've rested as the moon waned and expressed yourself as it waxed, you may find that you are flowing with the full moon.

If you've pushed through the waning phase and stifled the waxing phase, you may feel frustrated.

MOVE SOME ENERGY: Go for a drive with the windows down, dance, breathe deeply, or sing.

FINISH UP: Clean your space and check things off your to-do list—especially things you've been putting off. This can help move stagnant energy.

EMOTE AND EXPRESS: Give a voice to your emotions—journal, paint, draw, talk, cry, yell—allow your emotional body to surface.

DIVINE AND REVEAL: Your intuition may be clearest at the full moon. Decision-making and divination can be highly effective at this time. Some believe the full moon is not a good time for decisions, but try it and see what you think.

BATHE: Epsom salt baths or swimming are fabulous ways to neutralize the moon's energy.

LET YOURSELF BE A LUNATIC: Literally. Go outside and scream, "I AM A LUNATIC!" Then cackle wildly (Trust! It's okay! Give it a try).

You may prefer to howl at the moon. This is also acceptable and highly encouraged.

JULY 2023

*Enliven your spiritual and energetic frequencies
with apatite, turquoise, or kyanite.*

	SUNDAY	MONDAY	TUESDAY
	25	26 First Quarter ◗	27
	2	3 Full Moon ○ ♋︎	4
	9 Last Quarter ◖	10	11
	16	17 New Moon ● ♋︎	18
	23	24	25 First Quarter ◗
	30	31	★ Lughnasadh (Fixed Date)
			1 Full Moon ○

WEDNESDAY	THURSDAY	FRIDAY	SATURDAY
28	29	Neptune Retrograde Begins (Ends Dec. 6) 30	1
5	6	7	8
12	13	14	15
19	20	21	22 ☉ Sun enters Leo ♌
26	27	28	29
2	3	4	5

JULY 2023

MONDAY, JULY 3
Full Moon ○ in Capricorn ♑ 7:39 AM EDT

TUESDAY, JULY 4
► Moon void of course begins 12:45 PM EDT
Moon enters Aquarius ♒ 1:30 PM EDT

WEDNESDAY, JULY 5

THURSDAY, JULY 6
► Moon void of course begins 9:42 AM EDT
Moon enters Pisces ♓ 1:32 PM EDT

FRIDAY, JULY 7

- White Horse -
The unbridled power of
the full moon.

SATURDAY, JULY 8
► Moon void of course begins 2:22 PM EDT
Moon enters Aries ♈ 3:19 PM EDT

SUNDAY, JULY 9
Last Quarter ◑ 9:48 PM EDT

Carve a small white candle with symbols
of your desires. Set it out under the full
moon and let it burn all the way down.

JULY 2023

MONDAY, JULY 10
► Moon void of course begins 7:11 PM EDT
Moon enters Taurus ♉ 7:55 PM EDT

TUESDAY, JULY 11

WEDNESDAY, JULY 12

THURSDAY, JULY 13
► Moon void of course begins 2:11 AM EDT
Moon enters Gemini ♊ 3:26 AM EDT

FRIDAY, JULY 14

SATURDAY, JULY 15
► Moon void of course begins 8:35 AM EDT
Moon enters Cancer ♋ 1:13 PM EDT

SUNDAY, JULY 16

Rose

**The full bloom of
your spirit**

JULY 2023

MONDAY, JULY 17
New Moon ● ♋ 2:32 PM EDT
➤ Moon void of course begins 11:06 PM EDT

TUESDAY, JULY 18
Moon enters Leo ♌ 12:39 AM EDT

WEDNESDAY, JULY 19

THURSDAY, JULY 20
➤ Moon void of course begins 10:08 AM EDT
Moon enters Virgo ♍ 1:13 PM EDT

FRIDAY, JULY 21

SATURDAY, JULY 22
☉ Sun enters Leo ♌ 9:50 PM EDT
♀℞ Venus Retrograde July 22 – Sept. 3

SUNDAY, JULY 23
➤ Moon void of course begins 12:06 AM EDT
Moon enters Libra ♎ 1:54 AM EDT
Chiron Retrograde July 23 – Dec. 26
100 days till Halloween!

*Sprinkle crushed mugwort, sage, and
periwinkle to cast a magic circle or burn
these herbs as full moon divination incense.*

JULY 2023

MONDAY, JULY 24

TUESDAY, JULY 25
► Moon void of course begins 11:05 AM EDT
Moon enters Scorpio ♏ 12:55 PM EDT
First Quarter ◐ 6:07 PM EDT

WEDNESDAY, JULY 26

THURSDAY, JULY 27
► Moon void of course begins 8:54 PM EDT
Moon enters Sagittarius ♐ 8:24 PM EDT

FRIDAY, JULY 28

SATURDAY, JULY 29
► Moon void of course begins 7:51 PM EDT
Moon enters Capricorn ♑ 11:44 PM EDT

SUNDAY, JULY 30

Howl
at the moon

JULY/AUGUST 2023

MONDAY, JULY 31
➤ Moon void of course begins 10:13 PM EDT
Moon enters Aquarius ♒ 11:58 PM EDT

TUESDAY, AUGUST 1
★ Lughnasadh (Fixed Festival Date)
Full Moon ○ ♒ 2:32 PM EDT

WEDNESDAY, AUGUST 2
➤ Moon void of course begins 5:15 PM EDT
Moon enters Pisces ♓ 11:05 PM EDT

Place peonies on your altar to soothe the effects of the moon. Or wear a necklace made of dried peony root strung like beads.

THURSDAY, AUGUST 3

FRIDAY, AUGUST 4
➤ Moon void of course begins 9:21 PM EDT
Moon enters Aries ♈ 11:19 PM EDT

SATURDAY, AUGUST 5

SUNDAY, AUGUST 6

Sandalwood is a powerful full moon incense to steady and attune your energy.

In my defense,
the moon was full.

Protect yourself from werewolves
with aconite (wolfsbane).

VISION & INTENTION
Gather your power. You are whole.

REFLECTION
What's working for you? What's not?

GOALS & ACTIONS
What does your magic need from you?

INTUITION
Accept all phases of yourself & begin again.

- Clary Sage & Rowanberry -
Enhancing psychic & intuitive powers.

THIS MONTH:

Full Moon in Aquarius: August 1
Lughnasadh: August 1-7
New Moon in Leo: August 16
Sun enters Virgo: August 23
Mercury ℞: August 23- Sept. 15
Uranus ℞: August 28 -Jan. 27, 2024
Full Blue Moon)(: August 30

- Wheat & Grains -
Abundance

AUGUST

INTUITION

Look at the moon to connect to your own
guiding light and the knowing within yourself.

Cultivate the feeling that you are capable.

Craft protective brooms with bundles of pennyroyal, heather, or rue. Use these brooms to sweep your altar.

Use ash twigs to craft magically protective wands, wreaths, and brooms.

Make Life Magical

WANING GIBBOUS MOON
CREATING MAGIC WITH MOON ARTS AND CRAFTS

The moon has inspired the arts and human expression for thousands of years.

Any moon phase is a good time to make moon-art! But the waning gibbous moon can be extra special for crafting, as this moon is auspicious for studying, finding inspiration in nature, and discovering your sense of purpose—just like crafts.

CRAFT RITUALS: Set the intention of what you desire as you plan your moon-craft project. Find materials that symbolize your spellwork and manifestations for this next moon cycle.

As you craft, ask to channel the power and wisdom of the moon. Create in silence, or repeat a moon mantra, for example: *Dark to light, the power of the night. Wax and wane, release and gain.*

When finished, place your moon craft in a location of reverence, such as on your altar.

Stitch Witchery: Whether you sew, embroider, or do quilting, you can work moon-themed motifs, spirals, and lunar magic into anything you make. Experiment with "moon colors" and symbolism in silver, gold, and blue.

Jewelry and Adornments: Try your hand at beading with shiny moon crystals and lunar accouterments. Pearls, onyx, silver, quartz, and moonstone all symbolize the magic of the moon.

Stamps: Carve a potato with the triple moon, a spiral, or moon-phase motif. Then use fabric paint to stamp bands of lunar spellwork at the hems of dish towels, aprons, an altar cloth, special paper, clothing, or ritual tools.

Wreaths and Altar Decorations: Create lunar deity statues or other special symbolisms for your altar or to adorn a moon-shaped wreath.

AUGUST 2023

	SUNDAY	MONDAY	TUESDAY
			★Lughnasadh (Fixed Date) 1 Full Moon ○ ≈
	30	31	
		★Lughnasadh 2:21 PM EST 7	8 Last Quarter ◑
	6		
	13	14	15
	20	21	22
	27	28	29

Lemon Balm
(Melissa)

WEDNESDAY	THURSDAY	FRIDAY	SATURDAY
2	3	4	5
9	10	11	12
16 New Moon ● ♌ ☉ Sun enters Virgo ♍	17	18	19
23	24 First Quarter ◐	25	26
30 Full Moon ○ ♓	31	1	2

AUGUST 2023

MONDAY, AUGUST 7
► Moon void of course begins 12:13 AM EDT
Moon enters Taurus ♉ 2:24 AM EDT
★ Lughnasadh (Astronomical Date) 2:21 PM EDT

TUESDAY, AUGUST 8
Last Quarter ◑ 6:28 AM EDT

WEDNESDAY, AUGUST 9
► Moon void of course begins 6:39 AM EDT
Moon enters Gemini ♊ 9:05 AM EDT

THURSDAY, AUGUST 10

FRIDAY, AUGUST 11
► Moon void of course begins 1:27 PM EDT
Moon enters Cancer ♋ 6:52 PM EDT

SATURDAY, AUGUST 12

SUNDAY, AUGUST 13

- Poppy -
Sleep, peace, and
moon power

AUGUST 2023

MONDAY, AUGUST 14
► Moon void of course begins 3:46 AM EDT
Moon enters Leo ♌ 6:36 AM EDT

TUESDAY, AUGUST 15

WEDNESDAY, AUGUST 16
New Moon ● in Leo ♌ 5:38 AM EDT
► Moon void of course begins 5:38 AM EDT
Moon enters Virgo ♍ 7:14 PM EDT

THURSDAY, AUGUST 17

FRIDAY, AUGUST 18

SATURDAY, AUGUST 19
► Moon void of course begins 4:51 AM EDT
Moon enters Libra ♎ 7:53 AM EDT

SUNDAY, AUGUST 20

- Tourmaline, Tiger's Eye, Turquoise -
Meditate with or carry these stones to
hear the subtleties of your intuition.

AUGUST 2023

MONDAY, AUGUST 21
▸ Moon void of course begins 4:31 PM EDT
Moon enters Scorpio ♏ 7:22 PM EDT

TUESDAY, AUGUST 22

WEDNESDAY, AUGUST 23
☉ Sun enters Virgo ♍ 5:01 AM EDT
☿℞ Mercury Retrograde Aug. 23 – Sept. 15

THURSDAY, AUGUST 24
▸ Moon void of course begins 1:10 AM EDT
Moon enters Sagittarius ♐ 4:07 AM EDT
First Quarter ◑ 5:57 AM EDT

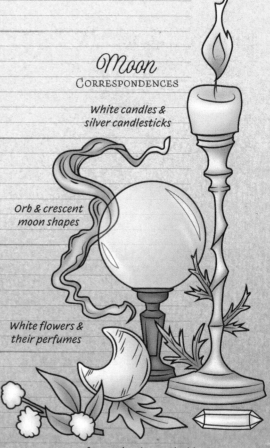

Moon
CORRESPONDENCES

*White candles &
silver candlesticks*

*Orb & crescent
moon shapes*

*White flowers &
their perfumes*

FRIDAY, AUGUST 25

SATURDAY, AUGUST 26
▸ Moon void of course begins 7:56 AM EDT
Moon enters Capricorn ♑ 9:05 PM EDT

SUNDAY, AUGUST 27

*Luna can perform miracles on the blue moon.
Set an altar to honor Luna and ask for what you need.*

AUGUST/SEPTEMBER 2023

MONDAY, AUGUST 28
⛢℞ Uranus Retrograde Aug. 28 - Jan. 27, 2024
► Moon void of course begins 7:49 AM EDT
Moon enters Aquarius ♒ 10:32 AM EDT

TUESDAY, AUGUST 29
► Moon void of course begins 11:04 PM EDT

WEDNESDAY, AUGUST 30
Moon enters Pisces ♓ 9:56 AM EDT
Full Blue Moon ○ ♓ 9:36 PM EDT

THURSDAY, AUGUST 31

FRIDAY, SEPTEMBER 1
► Moon void of course begins 6:36 AM EDT
Moon enters Aries ♈ 9:25 AM EDT

SATURDAY, SEPTEMBER 2

SUNDAY, SEPTEMBER 3
► Moon void of course begins 7:57 AM EDT
Moon enters Taurus ♉ 11:00 AM EDT
♀℞ Venus Retrograde ends

Luna

*A Roman goddess
who personifies the
powers of the moon.*

VISION & INTENTION
Gather your power. You are whole.

REFLECTION
What's working for you? What's not?

GOALS & ACTIONS
What does your magic need from you?

INTUITION
Accept all phases of yourself & begin again.

- Round fruits, gourds, & squash -
The abundance of the earth and the power of the moon.

THIS MONTH:

Venus ℞ ends: September 3
Jupiter ℞: September 4 - December 30
New Moon in Virgo: September 14
Mercury ℞ ends: September 15
Mabon (Autumnal Equinox): September 23
Sun enters Libra: September 23
Full Moon in Aries: September 29

Fruit will "shrump up" if picked on the waning moon. Always harvest on the full moon.

SEPTEMBER

RELEASE

Look at the moon to let go of situations that are holding you back.

Courageously choose what you desire.

"Letting Go" doesn't mean pretending it didn't matter or didn't happen.

"Letting Go" means witnessing and accepting all of your feelings, then choosing what you want to focus on next.

Tourmaline can help you accept where you might benefit from change.

To calm and release your emotions, bathe with salt and herbs like hyssop, lavender, calendula, or chamomile.

LAST QUARTER MOON
RELEASING WITH MOON WATER

Do this work during any waning moon or on the full moon in September.

The last quarter moon holds a diminishing power. Change is hard, and the power of the waning moon's decaying energy can help make changes and releases a little easier. It's often the emotions of change that hurt. And since the moon corresponds to both water and emotions, these things together make for potent magic.

Write a list of the things you want to release—physically as well as emotionally—like thoughts, habits, resentments, mistakes, or patterns.

WITH TEARS: When performing these spells, allow yourself to deeply feel the emotions of letting go. Cry if possible—a release of water.

IN THE BATH: Soak while feeling or speaking what you wish to release. Feel the energy leave your body and absorb into the water. As the bath drains, let the emotions release along with it.

IN THE RAIN: Use white chalk to write what you wish to release on stones (or directly on the ground). Place the stones in the rain, then watch as the writing dissipates. Alternately, stand in the rain and allow the energy to wash away.

AT THE WATER'S EDGE: Gaze at the reflection of the waning moon on the water. Speak what you wish to release. Place your feet in the water and allow the energy to move through you, into the water, and to the reflection of the moon.

WITH A CHALICE: Fill a silver chalice with water. Light a candle. Speak the energies that you wish to release. Extinguish the flame in the chalice's water. Pour the water out at a crossroads or onto the bare earth.

SEPTEMBER 2023

- Moon Hare or Moon Rabbit -
Asian and Native American folklores
tell of a rabbit in the moon.

SUNDAY	MONDAY	TUESDAY
27	28	29
3	4	5
10	11	12
17	18	19
24	25	26

TSUKIMI
is a moon viewing festival to celebrate the autumn harvest moon.

WEDNESDAY	THURSDAY	FRIDAY	SATURDAY
30 Full Moon ○	**31**	**1**	**2**
6 Last Quarter ◑	**7**	**8**	**9**
13	**14** New Moon ● ♍	**15**	**16**
20	**21**	**22** First Quarter ◐ Tsukimi Moon Festival	**23** ⊙ Sun enters Libra ★ Mabon (Autumnal Equinox)
27	**28**	**29** Full Moon ○ ♈	**30**

SEPTEMBER 2023

MONDAY, SEPTEMBER 4
♃ ℞ Jupiter Retrograde September 4 – December 30

TUESDAY, SEPTEMBER 5
► Moon void of course begins 12:46 PM EDT
Moon enters Gemini ♊ 4:07 PM EDT

WEDNESDAY, SEPTEMBER 6
Last Quarter ◑ 6:21 PM EDT

THURSDAY, SEPTEMBER 7
► Moon void of course begins 6:22 PM EDT

FRIDAY, SEPTEMBER 8
Moon enters Cancer ♋ 1:00 AM EDT

SATURDAY, SEPTEMBER 9

SUNDAY, SEPTEMBER 10
► Moon void of course begins 8:47 AM EDT
Moon enters Leo ♌ 12:36 PM EDT

*Burn star anise and apple wood to release and
clear energy on the Autumnal Equinox.*

SEPTEMBER 2023

MONDAY, SEPTEMBER 11

TUESDAY, SEPTEMBER 12
► Moon void of course begins 11:06 AM EDT

WEDNESDAY, SEPTEMBER 13
Moon enters Virgo ♍ 1:18 AM EDT

THURSDAY, SEPTEMBER 14
New Moon ● in Virgo ♍ 9:40 PM EDT

FRIDAY, SEPTEMBER 15
☿℞ Mercury Retrograde Ends
► Moon void of course begins 9:49 AM EDT
Moon enters Libra ♎ 1:44 PM EDT

SATURDAY, SEPTEMBER 16

SUNDAY, SEPTEMBER 17
► Moon void of course begins 9:06 PM EDT

INSIGHT & RELEASE

Jet

Henbane

Blackthorn

WANING MOON

SEPTEMBER 2023

MONDAY, SEPTEMBER 18
Moon enters Scorpio ♏ 12:58 AM EDT

TUESDAY, SEPTEMBER 19

WEDNESDAY, SEPTEMBER 20
► Moon void of course begins 6:21 AM EDT
Moon enters Sagittarius ♐ 10:06 AM EDT

THURSDAY, SEPTEMBER 21

FRIDAY, SEPTEMBER 22
First Quarter ◑ 3:32 PM EDT
► Moon void of course begins 3:32 PM EDT
Moon enters Capricorn ♑ 4:20 PM EDT

SATURDAY, SEPTEMBER 23
☉ Sun enters Libra ♎ 2:50 AM EDT
★ Mabon (Autumnal Equinox) 2:50 AM EDT

SUNDAY, SEPTEMBER 24
► Moon void of course begins 4:05 PM EDT
Moon enters Aquarius ♒ 7:29 PM EDT

Chang'e
Chinese Goddess of the Moon

Honor Chang'e with round autumn nuts and fruits like hazelnuts, chestnuts, and persimmons.

SEPTEMBER/OCTOBER 2023

MONDAY, SEPTEMBER 25

TUESDAY, SEPTEMBER 26
▸ Moon void of course begins 8:39 AM EDT
Moon enters Pisces ♓ 8:18 PM EDT

WEDNESDAY, SEPTEMBER 27

THURSDAY, SEPTEMBER 28
▸ Moon void of course begins 4:58 PM EDT
Moon enters Aries ♈ 8:17 PM EDT

FRIDAY, SEPTEMBER 29
Full Moon ○ in Aries ♈ 5:58 AM EDT
★ Tsukimi Moon Viewing Festival

SATURDAY, SEPTEMBER 30
▸ Moon void of course begins 5:49 PM EDT
Moon enters Taurus ♉ 9:18 PM EDT

SUNDAY, OCTOBER 1

Rabbit

Eat mochi or dango to celebrate the Tsukimi moon festival.

VISION & INTENTION
Gather your power. You are whole.

REFLECTION
What's working for you? What's not?

GOALS & ACTIONS
What does your magic need from you?

INTUITION
Accept all phases of yourself & begin again.

- Bats & Ravens -
Wisdom of the dark

- Parsley -
Spiritual protection

THIS MONTH:

Pluto ℞ ends: October 10
New Moon in Libra: October 14
Annular Solar Eclipse: October 14
Sun enters Scorpio: October 23
Full Moon in Taurus: October 28
Partial Lunar Eclipse: October 28
Samhain: October 31-November 7

Burn mugwort and patchouli to raise spiritual energy

- Pumpkins -
Moon power and magic

OCTOBER
SPIRIT OF THE WITCH
Look at the moon to increase your psychic awareness and learn from the past.

Listen closely to your intuition.

FIRE: What actions make you feel heavy?

WATER: What emotions feel stuck and in need of release?

AIR: What unhelpful thoughts or beliefs are lurking in the shadow?

EARTH: What items or habits are holding you back?

SPIRIT: What have you been denying?

- Heather & Labradorite -
Spiritual protection and
enlightenment

WANING CRESCENT MOON
DIVINATION WITH THE CRONE

Do this "shadow work" on any waning crescent moon or on the full moon in October.

The waning crescent, the last sliver of light before the moon falls to darkness, is an auspicious time for delving into the shadow self, the subconscious, and all that is hidden beneath the surface. This moon represents the Crone goddess, the wisdom of the elder witch, or the wisdom of your own "elder" within.

While the previous spell dealt with emotions on the surface, we also hold emotions in the shadow. These are the things we have not yet felt or allowed ourselves to accept. Performing "shadow-work" can uncover what may lurk in the darkness of your own power.

THINGS YOU'LL NEED: Tarot cards or another form of divination (oracle cards, rune stones, a pendulum, the moon's reflection on water for scrying, or a notebook and pen to free-write).

Optional: Black candles. A dark incense such as frankincense, sloe berries, or cedar.

PERFORM THE SPELL: Walk, dance, or spiral counterclockwise (widdershins) and backwards. Or circle your hands widdershins until you feel your energy shift. You can greatly heighten the power of the ritual if you walk backwards on a wooded path, especially to a crossroads, but go slowly and use extreme caution if you do so.

As you circle or walk, chant:

Into the shadows to see the Crone.
While the night is dark, I am not alone.

Light your candle(s) and incense if desired. Then use your divination tool to ask the Crone the questions on the facing page.

OCTOBER 2023

	SUNDAY	MONDAY	TUESDAY
	1	2	3
	8	9	10
	15	16	17
	22	23 ⊙ Sun enters Scorpio	24
	29	30	31 ★Samhain (fixed date)

WEDNESDAY	THURSDAY	FRIDAY	SATURDAY
4	5	6 Last Quarter ◐	7 Annular Solar Eclipse
11	12	13	14 New Moon ● ♎
18	19	20	21 First Quarter ◑ Partial Lunar Eclipse
25	26	27	28 Full Moon ○ ♉
1	2	3	4

OCTOBER 2023

MONDAY, OCTOBER 2
► Moon void of course begins 9:20 PM EDT

TUESDAY, OCTOBER 3
Moon enters Gemini ♊ 1:03 AM EDT

WEDNESDAY, OCTOBER 4

THURSDAY, OCTOBER 5
► Moon void of course begins 2:34 AM EDT
Moon enters Cancer ♋ 8:32 AM EDT

FRIDAY, OCTOBER 6
Last Quarter ◑ 9:48 AM EDT

SATURDAY, OCTOBER 7
► Moon void of course begins 3:12 PM EDT
Moon enters Leo ♌ 7:24 PM EDT

SUNDAY, OCTOBER 8

Stir counterclockwise during the waning moon to release and reflect.

Make dark moon water with vervain and vetivert root. Use it as an offering to Cerridwen or as a blessing water to release things.

OCTOBER 2023

MONDAY, OCTOBER 9

TUESDAY, OCTOBER 10
▸ Moon void of course begins 5:37 AM EDT
Moon enters Virgo ♍ 8:02 AM EDT

WEDNESDAY, OCTOBER 11
♇ℝ Pluto Retrograde ends

THURSDAY, OCTOBER 12
▸ Moon void of course begins 4:10 PM EDT
Moon enters Libra ♎ 8:22 PM EDT

FRIDAY, OCTOBER 13

SATURDAY, OCTOBER 14
New Moon ● in Libra ♎ 1:55 PM EDT
Annular Solar Eclipse ♎ 2:00 PM EDT

SUNDAY, OCTOBER 15
▸ Moon void of course begins 3:01 AM EDT
Moon enters Scorpio ♏ 7:04 AM EDT

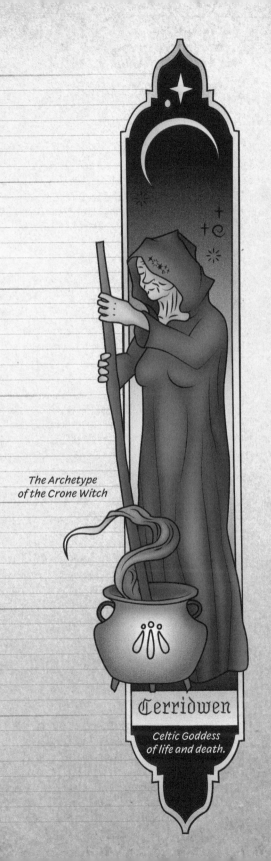

*The Archetype
of the Crone Witch*

Cerridwen

*Celtic Goddess
of life and death.*

OCTOBER 2023

MONDAY, OCTOBER 16

TUESDAY, OCTOBER 17
► Moon void of course begins 11:44 AM EDT
Moon enters Sagittarius ♐ 3:36 PM EDT

WEDNESDAY, OCTOBER 18

THURSDAY, OCTOBER 19
► Moon void of course begins 3:02 PM EDT
Moon enters Capricorn ♑ 9:55 PM EDT

FRIDAY, OCTOBER 20

SATURDAY, OCTOBER 21
First Quarter ◑ 11:29 PM EDT

SUNDAY, OCTOBER 22
► Moon void of course begins 2:00 AM EDT
Moon enters Aquarius ♒ 2:06 AM EDT

*Gaze into a dark stone like obsidian
or into a black bowl of water to
divine wisdom from the darkness.*

OCTOBER 2023

MONDAY, OCTOBER 23
☉ Sun enters Scorpio ♏ 12:24 PM
► Moon void of course begins 3:04 PM EDT

TUESDAY, OCTOBER 24
Moon enters Pisces ♓ 4:33 AM EDT

WEDNESDAY, OCTOBER 25

THURSDAY, OCTOBER 26
► Moon void of course begins 2:39 AM EDT
Moon enters Aries ♈ 6:02 AM EDT

FRIDAY, OCTOBER 27

SATURDAY, OCTOBER 28
► Moon void of course begins 4:20 AM EDT
Moon enters Taurus ♉ 7:44 AM EDT
Partial Lunar Eclipse ♉ 4:15 PM EDT
Full Moon ○ in Taurus ♉ 4:24 PM EDT

SUNDAY, OCTOBER 29

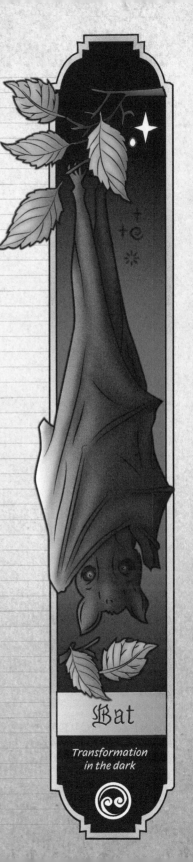

Bat

*Transformation
in the dark*

OCTOBER/NOVEMBER 2023

MONDAY, OCTOBER 30
► Moon void of course begins 7:36 AM EDT
Moon enters Gemini ♊ 11:08 AM EDT

TUESDAY, OCTOBER 31
★ Samhain (Fixed Festival Date)

WEDNESDAY, NOVEMBER 1
► Moon void of course begins 8:36 AM EDT
Moon enters Cancer ♋ 5:30 PM EDT

THURSDAY, NOVEMBER 2

- Thorns & Brambles -
Protection & Regeneration

FRIDAY, NOVEMBER 3
► Moon void of course begins 11:28 PM EDT

SATURDAY, NOVEMBER 4
Saturn ℞ ends
Moon enters Leo ♌ 3:21 AM EDT

SUNDAY, NOVEMBER 5
Last Quarter ◑ 3:37 AM EST

Drink rose hip tea to attune
to your psychic powers.

Spiral or dance counterclockwise under the waning
moon to release what no longer serves you.

VISION & INTENTION
Gather your power. You are whole.

REFLECTION
What's working for you? What's not?

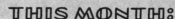

GOALS & ACTIONS
What does your magic need from you?

INTUITION
Accept all phases of yourself & begin again.

- Wormwood & Nutmeg -
Psychic Powers

- Owl -
Wisdom & Intuition

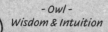

THIS MONTH:

Samhain: October 31-November 7
Saturn ℞ ends: November 4
New Moon in Scorpio: November 13
Sun Enters Sagittarius: November 22
Full Moon in Gemini: November 27

- Amber -
Forgiveness and trust in yourself

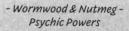

NOVEMBER

TRANSFORMATION

Release past and future expectations
and experience the peace of "now."

Transcend through forgiveness of self.

Acorns

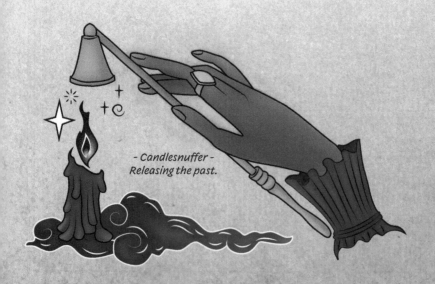

- Candlesnuffer -
Releasing the past.

THE DARK MOON
A CLASSIC "CORD CUTTING" RITUAL

Perform this spell during a dark moon, before any hint of the returning light of the new moon.

Cord cutting is a classic witch's rite, often performed to cut the ties between yourself and another person, most notably, a lover. However, you can use this ritual to "cut the cord" between yourself and whatever you wish to release.

The past two spells have dealt with letting go. While you may feel some relief and release—you might also still feel stuck on a thing or two, and that's okay. Some energies are hard to let go of, even when we desperately wish to let go. And the dark moon is the perfect void to release into.

THINGS YOU'LL NEED: Two small spell candles, colors of your choice. One to represent you, and one to represent the energy you wish to detach from. A length of natural twine (hemp, jute,

cotton, or even a long length of dried grass). A fire-safe cauldron or location to burn things.

Perform this spell outside under the dark moon or indoors with the windows open.

CAST THE SPELL: Set up the two spell candles securely, a few inches from each other. Tie the twine around both of the candles several times, in a counterclockwise direction.

Then, light the candles. Allow them to burn down, burning the twine (the bond) along with them. Watch the candles and threads as they burn. Chant if you like, "The ties that bind, no longer mine. I release this bond, here and beyond."

Allow any memories or emotions to surface, then breathe them out towards the flame. Let the candles burn out. Bury any remnants of the spell in the ground or in a pot of earth.

NOVEMBER 2023

Folklore from Chinese, African, and Native American traditions tell tales of a toad or frog in the moon.

SUNDAY	MONDAY	TUESDAY
		★ Samhain (Fixed Date)
29	30	31
		★ Samhain 11:18 AM
5 Last Quarter ◑	6	7
★ Diwali		
12	13 New Moon ● ♏	14
19	20 First Quarter ◑	21
26	27 Full Moon ○ ♊	28

Gaze at the moon until you see a toad, then make a wish for transformation.

WEDNESDAY	THURSDAY	FRIDAY	SATURDAY
1	2	3	4
8	9	10	11
15	16	17	18
22 ⊙ Sun Enters Sagittarius	23	24	25
29	30	1	2

NOVEMBER 2023

MONDAY, NOVEMBER 6
► Moon void of course begins 2:25 AM EST
Moon enters Virgo ♍ 2:39 PM EST

TUESDAY, NOVEMBER 7
★ Samhain (Astronomical Date) 11:18 AM EST

WEDNESDAY, NOVEMBER 8
► Moon void of course begins 11:55 PM EST

THURSDAY, NOVEMBER 9
Moon enters Libra ♎ 3:08 AM EST

FRIDAY, NOVEMBER 10

SATURDAY, NOVEMBER 11
► Moon void of course begins 10:05 AM EST
Moon enters Scorpio ♏ 1:39 PM EST

SUNDAY, NOVEMBER 12

"Raising my cup, I greet the bright
moon and turn to my shadow
which makes us three."

Drinking Alone Under the Moon
Li Bai, AD 743 (translated excerpt)

NOVEMBER 2023

MONDAY, NOVEMBER 13
New Moon ● ♏ 4:27 AM EST
► Moon void of course begins 6:03 PM EST
Moon enters Sagittarius ♐ 9:23 PM EST

TUESDAY, NOVEMBER 14

WEDNESDAY, NOVEMBER 15
► Moon void of course begins 5:57 PM EST

THURSDAY, NOVEMBER 16
Moon enters Capricorn ♑ 2:41 AM EST

FRIDAY, NOVEMBER 17

SATURDAY, NOVEMBER 18
► Moon void of course begins 3:27 AM EST
Moon enters Aquarius ♒ 6:27 AM EST

SUNDAY, NOVEMBER 19

REST &
REGENERATE

Jet

Belladonna

Blackthorn

Onyx

DARK
MOON

NOVEMBER 2023

MONDAY, NOVEMBER 20
First Quarter ◑ 5:50 AM EST
► Moon void of course begins 5:50 AM EST
Moon enters Pisces ♓ 9:29 AM EST

TUESDAY, NOVEMBER 21

WEDNESDAY, NOVEMBER 22
☉ Sun enters Sagittarius ♐ 9:02 AM EST
► Moon void of course begins 10:10 AM EST
Moon enters Aries ♈ 12:19 PM EST

THURSDAY, NOVEMBER 23

FRIDAY, NOVEMBER 24
► Moon void of course begins 12:40 PM EST
Moon enters Taurus ♉ 3:29 PM EST

SATURDAY, NOVEMBER 25

SUNDAY, NOVEMBER 26
► Moon void of course begins 4:52 PM EST
Moon enters Gemini ♊ 7:40 PM EST

Clear your broom and ritual tools with the smoke of cedar, fennel, hyssop, and rosemary, or with a sprinkle of salt water.

NOVEMBER/DECEMBER 2023

MONDAY, NOVEMBER 27
Full Moon ○ in Gemini Ⅱ 4:16 AM EST

TUESDAY, NOVEMBER 28
► Moon void of course begins 8:03 PM EST

WEDNESDAY, NOVEMBER 29
Moon enters Cancer ♋ 1:54 AM EST

THURSDAY, NOVEMBER 30

FRIDAY, DECEMBER 1
► Moon void of course begins 8:07 AM EST
Moon enters Leo ♌ 11:00 AM EST

SATURDAY, DECEMBER 2

SUNDAY, DECEMBER 3
► Moon void of course begins 9:11 PM EST
Moon enters Virgo ♍ 10:50 PM EST

Hellebore

*Banishing &
Protection*

VISION & INTENTION
Gather your power. You are whole.

REFLECTION
What's working for you? What's not?

GOALS & ACTIONS
What does your magic need from you?

INTUITION
Accept all phases of yourself & begin again.

Carry a bloodstone to ground your energy as you step into the unknown.

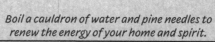

Boil a cauldron of water and pine needles to renew the energy of your home and spirit.

THIS MONTH:

Neptune ℞ ends: December 6
New Moon in Sagittarius: December 12
Mercury ℞ begins Dec. 13 and ends Jan 1
Yule (Winter Solstice): December 21
Sun Enters Capricorn: December 21
Full Moon in Cancer: December 26
Jupiter ℞ ends: December 30

- Evergreens-
Pine, Juniper,
and Cypress.

Immortality and the
cycles of life and death.

DECEMBER

RENEWAL

Rest, recharge, and surrender to the
infinite possibility of the unknown.

Trust that the light will return.

*Burn sandalwood and lavender
to enhance your spirit work.*

*Gaze at the stars on
a moonless night.*

*Drink black tea with mugwort,
thyme, and wormwood to
heighten your psychic awareness.*

The End is the Beginning
Finding the Wisdom in the Dark

The dark moon is a time to surrender to what is. This doesn't mean giving up, but letting go, and preparing for new possibilities when the light of the moon returns and the cycle begins again.

The energy of the dark moon suggests that there is wisdom in the space between the moons. There's a reason why the moon doesn't shine every night—the darkness is essential in magic.

THINGS YOU'LL NEED: A dark space to sit in silence. Thirteen candles set in a circle to represent each of the moons of the year.

CAST THE SPELL: Light all thirteen candles, then cast your circle around them. Go within the circle, and allow yourself several moments of silence and meditation. Think about the year and the thirteen moons that have passed. The memories may still be strong in your mind, but in actuality, the past—even the recent past—no longer exists. It is done.

One by one, blow out each candle while you say or think a memory from your year. It's up to you whether they are your favorite memories, your least favorite, or a mix. Let them all neutralize.

Once all of the candles have been extinguished, allow yourself a moment in the pitch darkness. Then, just see what comes to you.

What are you feeling in the dark? What does it represent to you, both seasonally and personally? What is your relationship to the darkness of your year? How would you like that to grow or change as the moon's light slowly returns?

After you've said your piece, listen deeply. What do you hear? What is the wisdom of the dark saying back to you?

DECEMBER 2023

For spiritual protection, anoint candles with powerful oils like patchouli, vetivert, and cloves.

	SUNDAY	MONDAY	TUESDAY
	26	27 Full Moon ○	28
	3	4	5 Last Quarter ◑
	10	11	12 New Moon ● ♐
	17	18	19 First Quarter ◐
	24	25	26 Full Moon ○ ♋
	31	1	2

WEDNESDAY	THURSDAY	FRIDAY	SATURDAY
29	30	1	2
6	7	8	9
13	14	15	16
20	21 ★ Yule (Winter Solstice) ☉ Sun Enters Capricorn	22	23
27	28	29	30
3 Last Quarter ☽	4	5	6

DECEMBER 2023

MONDAY, DECEMBER 4

TUESDAY, DECEMBER 5
Last Quarter ◖ 12:49 AM EST

WEDNESDAY, DECEMBER 6
► Moon void of course begins 8:50 AM EST
Moon enters Libra ♎ 1:35 AM EST
♆℞ Neptune Retrograde ends

THURSDAY, DECEMBER 7

FRIDAY, DECEMBER 8
► Moon void of course begins 8:50 PM EST
Moon enters Scorpio ♏ 10:35 PM EST

SATURDAY, DECEMBER 9

SUNDAY, DECEMBER 10

*Honor Hecate with dark plants from her garden,
like aconite, belladonna, hellebore, mugwort, and asphodel.
Use caution as many of her favorites are poisonous.*

DECEMBER 2023

MONDAY, DECEMBER 11
► Moon void of course begins 3:57 AM EST
Moon enters Sagittarius ♐ 6:11 AM EST

TUESDAY, DECEMBER 12
New Moon ● in Sagittarius ♐ 6:32 PM EST

WEDNESDAY, DECEMBER 13
☿℞ Mercury Retrograde Dec. 13 - Jan. 1, 2024
► Moon void of course begins 1:49 AM EST
Moon enters Capricorn ♑ 10:31 AM EST

THURSDAY, DECEMBER 14

FRIDAY, DECEMBER 15
► Moon void of course begins 11:04 AM EST
Moon enters Aquarius ♒ 12:56 PM EST

SATURDAY, DECEMBER 16

SUNDAY, DECEMBER 17
► Moon void of course begins 7:04 AM EST
Moon enters Pisces ♓ 2:58 PM EST

Hecate

Greek Goddess of magic, the moon, and the darkness.

DECEMBER 2023

MONDAY, DECEMBER 18

TUESDAY, DECEMBER 19
First Quarter ☽ 1:39 PM EST
► Moon void of course begins 4:03 PM EST
Moon enters Aries ♈ 5:47 PM EST

WEDNESDAY, DECEMBER 20

THURSDAY, DECEMBER 21
► Moon void of course begins 9:47 PM EST
Moon enters Taurus ♉ 9:50 PM EST
★ Yule (Winter Solstice) 10:27 PM EST
☉ Sun enters Capricorn ♑ 10:27 PM EST

FRIDAY, DECEMBER 22

SATURDAY, DECEMBER 23

SUNDAY, DECEMBER 24
► Moon void of course begins 1:40 AM EST
Moon enters Gemini ♊ 3:15 AM EST

Drink "spiral tea" with sweet sugar and dark flavors such as horehound, licorice, or chocolate.

DECEMBER 2023

MONDAY, DECEMBER 25

TUESDAY, DECEMBER 26
► Moon void of course begins 2:55 AM EST
Moon enters Cancer ♋ 10:15 AM EST
Full Moon ○ ♋ 7:33 PM EST
Chiron retrograde ends

WEDNESDAY, DECEMBER 27

THURSDAY, DECEMBER 28
► Moon void of course begins 5:57 PM EST
Moon enters Leo ♌ 7:23 PM EST

FRIDAY, DECEMBER 29

SATURDAY, DECEMBER 30
♃℞ Jupiter Retrograde ends

SUNDAY, DECEMBER 31
► Moon void of course begins 12:18 AM EST
Moon enters Virgo ♍ 6:53 AM EST

Walk a labyrinth or dance in circles to welcome the next phase of life.

Spirals
Life, Death, & Rebirth

Howl at the moon and move forward one space.

Forget you have power. Go back one space.

Try something new during the waxing moon. Skip ahead seven.

Gaze at the full moon through a hagstone. Skip ahead three spaces.

Ignore your intuition. Go back one space.

Discover Hecate's keys. Skip ahead nine spaces.

Resist change. Go back six.

View the full moonrise. Skip ahead three spaces.

Skip a turn.

Harvest on the full moon. Skip ahead three spaces.

IT'S JUST A PHASE!
(START HERE)
MOON SPIRAL

Use dice or cards numbered 1-6 to move around the board.
If an illustration touches your square, follow the instructions.

Gaze at the moon's reflection in water. Skip ahead four.

Burn agrimony, hyssop, and vetivert to banish unwanted cycles and patterns.

Look at the Moon!

Très Riches
Heures
du Duc de Berry
-
The Limbourg
Brothers
& their
associates
-
15th Century

Jessica Elliott
Color Assistant

Bollank
Color & Art Assistant

Fiona Horne
Editor of Magick
& Editor
FionaHorne.com

Wendy Ledger
Editor
WendyLedgerAuthor.com

Kae Marie
Denino Editor

THANK YOU!

About the Artist

Amy Cesari
(and her familiar, Cornelius)

Amy is an author and illustrator who loves animated musicals. She also likes watercolor painting, witchcraft, and walking on the beach in a really big sun hat.

Not only does she own every Nintendo game console ever made, she's earned several fancy diplomas and enjoys continued studies in various magical practices.

CONTACT AMY AND SEE MORE BOOKS, PRINTABLE PAGES, AND ART:

Amy@ColoringBookofShadows.com
ColoringBookofShadows.com

Made in the USA
Coppell, TX
13 December 2022

89057168R00096